TEEN SCIENCE FAIR SOURCEBOOK

*To past, present, and future student scientists at the Academy for Math,
Engineering and Sciences, an open access public school in Salt Lake City, Utah*

Acknowledgments

Special thanks to the many contributors who recognize that giving students the creative freedom to ask questions and fir
answers leads to self-motivated learning and scientific discovery. To the staff, teachers, and students of AMES High Scho
for inspiring the content and strategies shared in this book. To Dr. Al Church for creating a school of possibilities and f
giving me the opportunity to develop a student research program. Special thanks to Tammy Aho for suggesting that I wri
a book to help students with their research efforts. To Siya Xuza, Shannon Babb, and Erica David for sharing the
remarkable discoveries and stories as top student scientists. To the Salt Lake Valley Science and Engineering Fair f
allowing me to interview and photograph student scientists. To the Society for Science and the Public for answering n
questions and connecting me with some of the amazing young scientists featured in the book. To scientists from t
University of Utah for offering their expertise. To Natasha Hawley for contributing her knowledge and creative ideas to
aspects of the stats chapter. Thanks to my home editor and mom for being the "non-scientific" eyes and for helping ma
sure the information was fun and easy to follow. Thanks to my husband and to my children, Lindsey and Natalie, for the
patience and encouragement.

Library of Congress Cataloging-in-Publication Data

Vickers, Tanya M.
  Teen science fair sourcebook : winning school science fairs and national competitions /
Tanya M. Vickers.
    p. cm.
  Includes bibliographical references and index.
  Summary: "Provides helpful tips for entering local and national science competitions"—Provided by publisher.
  ISBN-13: 978-0-7660-2711-4
  ISBN-10: 0-7660-2711-2
  1. Science fairs—United States. 2. Science projects—Competitions—United States. 3. Science—Study and teaching
(Secondary)—United States. I. Title.
  Q182.4.V53 2009
  507.8—dc22   2008030779

Printed in the United States of America

10 9 8 7 6 5 4 3 2

Photo Credits: Breanne Anderson, p. 127; Central Valley Water Reclamation Facility, Utah; pp. 32; Courtesy of Society for Scier
and the Public, p. 118; Daniel Blakemore, pp. 93, 135; Erica David, p. 28; Gleb Kuznetsov, pp. 3, 57; Katy Schramm, p. 11
Kristan Jacobsen, p. 18; Martin Shields / Photo Researchers, Inc., p. 70; Photo courtesy of Homer Hickam, Jr., p. 13; Shann
Babb, pp. 3, 30, 135; Shutterstock, p. 70 (inset); Siyabulela Xuza, pp. 3, 25, 135; Skyler Chubak, pp. 23, 116, 123, 131 and 14
Tamara Anderson, p. 51; Tanya Vickers, pp. 7, 8, 11, 34, 46, 53, 63, 66, 95, 96, 114, 137, 139, 144.

Cover Photo: Shutterstock

TEEN SCIENCE FAIR SOURCEBOOK

Winning School Science Fairs and National Competitions

Tanya M. Vickers

Enslow Publishers, Inc.
40 Industrial Road
Box 398
Berkeley Heights, NJ 07922
USA
http://www.enslow.com

CONTENTS

●●●●●●●●●●●●●●●●●●●●

Student Research

> *When you're curious, you find lots of interesting*
> *things to do.*
> —Walt Disney

Research: It's an adventure into uncharted territory. Great adventures often begin with a mystery. In experimental research the mystery is a question that you find inspiring. When the experiments are done, you will have solved the mystery and have quite a story to tell.

There's no better way to learn about and enjoy science than to become a scientist. That's why most professional scientists choose a career in research, and that's why student scientists learn so much from doing a project. You will learn things from a research project that you cannot read in a textbook or see in a movie. So get excited! This will likely be one of the best learning experiences you will ever have.

When Students Become Scientists

Science includes the fields of chemistry, biology, math, physics, psychology, environmental studies, engineering, and computers. Science is about asking questions and gaining knowledge. It is also about making discoveries that will advance medicine or help preserve our environment. When students get involved in research, they experience the scientific method. In science class, the scientific method is often defined in a series of simple steps (as you will read in Chapter 4), yet science is so much more. The real value and meaning of science comes to life when

Even games can be a source of inspiration. These students designed experiments to study reaction time using a game very similar to "Perfection."

students ask questions, design experiments, and find answers. Most students report their discoveries at school or local science fairs. Says tenth-grader Mary Lovell, a student at AMES High School in Salt Lake City, Utah, "Doing a science fair project has finally opened up a different way of learning than the typical textbook and notes. Since elementary school we have

At the Regional Science Fair in Salt Lake City, Utah, a group of high school scientists started a friendly rivalry with a neighboring school. Students used math and physics formulas to cryptically write AMES > West.

done the same things over and over. It was finally something new."

Top middle and high school student scientists walk away from science contests with awards, free trips, and scholarships for their college educations. Often their research is published in scientific journals, and some student engineers even get the opportunity to file for a patent before turning eighteen years old.

What Are You Curious About?

Scientific research is an opportunity to ask the questions you want to answer. Almost anything goes, from studies on human or animal behavior to building a robot for household chores.

What are your hobbies, interests, and favorite school subjects? Finding scientific inspiration needs to start with you. The right project will fuel your curiosity and determination and keep you learning and working until the science fair. Start thinking about your project early, find the right idea, and use this book to guide you through every step of the science fair process. Figure 1.1 shows you how.

In the chapters that follow, you will find the tools and information needed to do a science fair project that is creative and original. Find out about the research adventures of other students around the country and learn about opportunities to travel and earn

FIGURE 1.1

Steps in the Science Fair Process

What are your interests?
Think about things you are familiar with, such as hobbies, sports, and favorite school subjects.

Ask a question… *that can be answered with experiments or imagine a device that could be engineered to solve a problem.*

Read… *what is known about your topic. Start with the newspaper, Internet, and familiar textbooks.*

Create a research plan.
This plan is the "how to" for your project.

Check competition rules and complete applications for science fairs you plan to enter.

Do the work…*and keep careful records in a* **notebook***.*
Organize data into **results** *that teachers and science fair judges can understand. Your results can include graphs, tables, flow charts, diagrams, and photographs.*

Write a research report *and use the report to create an artistic* **scientific poster** *that reveals what your project is about and what you learned.*

Prepare for the science fair.
Practice your presentation out loud. Consider entering other scientific competitions.

This student is interested in aviation and owns a radio-controlled airplane. His experiment involved making minor modifications to his airplane and then testing flight performance.

scholarships by participating in science fairs at the local, national, and international level.

Science is not just for the brainy. Science is for the curious and adventurous! Use the information in this book to make your project more than just another school assignment.

I have no special talents. I am only passionately curious.
—Albert Einstein

Inspiring Stories of Student Scientists

When you're 64, and looking back, will it be with regret for all those lost, wasted years? I hope not. Live a life of optimism and adventure.

—Homer Hickam, Jr., winner of the 1960 National Science Fair; Author, *Rocket Boys*

The Assignment Doer vs. the Young Scientist

How do you look at doing a research project? Your perspective is important. It's the biggest factor in determining how your project will turn out. Student scientists can be divided into two groups based on their perspective and motivation. They're either "assignment doers" or "young scientists." Young scientists find a project that suits their interests and personalities. They are motivated by more than grades. They have a need to know.

How do student scientists find the right idea, the one that will inspire, motivate, and drive them? Start looking for inspiration by reading about motivated young scientists who have had fun, become famous and, in some cases, made a career out of research.

Some of the "rocket boys" in 1959: Homer Hickam, Jr., Quentin Wilson, Roy Lee Cooke, and Jimmy O'Dell Carroll. They built this model rocket out of paper to study and think about fin sizes. *(Not pictured: Billy Rose and Sherman Siers.)*

Homer Hickam may be the most inspirational and famous science fair student in history. It was the Russian spacecraft *Sputnik*, orbiting through an October sky in Coalwood, West Virginia, that inspired Homer Hickam's interest in rockets. Homer was part of a team of six high school scientists, also known as the "rocket boys." The students were from a poor coal mining community where sons were expected to follow in their fathers' footsteps. Every part of life in Coalwood was tied to mining coal. Homer was stubborn, curious, and determined. He wanted to learn everything about rockets, and he wanted a life outside of Coalwood. Under Homer's leadership, the rocket boys built, launched, and tested rockets and turned their dreams into reality. They won the 1960 National Science Fair (currently known as the International Science and Engineering Fair).

Homer Hickam shares his amazing true story in *Rocket Boys*, an engaging autobiography. It is a must-read for all student scientists! In 1999, this very popular book was made into the movie *October Sky*. Shuffle the letters in *Rocket Boys* and you'll see they also spell *October Sky*.

Finding inspiration and working hard toward a dream changed Homer Hickam's life. He graduated from college and worked as a rocket engineer for NASA before becoming a successful author. In fact, all of the rocket boys went to college and started careers outside the mining community of Coalwood. Today, they continue to encourage students to take on challenges that others may say are impossible. This group of first-generation college graduates inspired a community to think differently about science and education.

The rest of this chapter highlights the research experiences of some other student scientists. Perhaps one of their stories will inspire you to find a question and look for answers.

Eyewitness Recall

LIZZY MCMULLIN (TENTH GRADE)

Second Place, Behavioral Sciences, 2006 Regional Science and Engineering Fair, Salt Lake City

As a high school sophomore, Lizzy McMullin was considering her future. She had always been interested in the criminal justice system, so she decided to use her science fair project as a way to learn more. Finding the right project didn't take long. Dozens of news articles about innocent individuals convicted of crimes based on eyewitness testimony captured her interest. DNA testing gave these people a second chance and revealed real concerns about the reliability of eyewitness testimony. This is how Lizzy decided to learn more about the accuracy of eyewitness recall. Her experiments involved staging a crime in several classrooms at her high school.

> I picked a project that was about something that had always interested me. Criminal justice and psychology are two things that I have considered studying in college. By doing this project I realized that I really liked the behavioral aspects of the project the most.

15

LIZZY'S EXPERIMENT

The high school literature class was in full swing when an unexpected visitor entered. It took only seconds for the visitor to commit the crime. Markers, erasers, and other items were removed from the front of the classroom, and the perpetrator vanished as quickly as she had appeared. This woman was a complete stranger. She was conspicuously dressed, wearing a hat, jacket, and sunglasses. You'd think that this unannounced entry would be noticed by a class of high school students. But was it? What did the students remember? Could they be truthful and accurate in their descriptions of this thief?

EXPERIMENTAL DESIGN BASICS

Lizzy's hypothesis was this: When witnesses are aware that a crime is in progress, they will provide more accurate descriptions of the criminal and events. She tested whether this hypothesis was true by setting up an experiment in her school.

Lizzy's witnesses were students from four literature classes at her high school:

- CONTROL CLASSROOMS: Students were told that a crime would occur in the classroom and later they would be asked to recall details about the crime and the perpetrator.

- EXPERIMENTAL CLASSROOMS: The students were not given any advanced warning that a theft would take place in their classroom. They were later asked to recall details about the crime and perpetrator.

Lizzy consulted with local police to come up with questions to ask her witnesses.

RESULTS

Lizzy's final research report concluded, "When observers (experimental classes) are not paying close attention to the things happening around them, they have only poor recollection of the details of a crime. Even more disturbing, many of the witnesses thought they were providing accurate information when they were not. Experimental results support the hypothesis. Eyewitness testimony is more accurate when individuals are aware of an impending crime."

JUST THE BEGINNING: HOW FAR COULD LIZZY TAKE THIS STUDY?

How many other questions and testing scenarios can you come up with? The results from one set of experiments can lead young scientists in new and unexpected directions. In the end, the project may actually involve testing multiple hypotheses.

Backyard Bamboo

HAYDEN GRIFFIN (FIFTH GRADE)

Many ideas come from everyday observations and curiosities. Hayden Griffin had always wondered about

The bamboo in Hayden's yard can grow 7.6 meters (25 feet) in one season! Hayden's experiment led him to the observation that on sunny, warm days growth can be measured in inches. On cold, cloudy days, he measured no change.

the bamboo growing just outside his back door. The school science fair gave him a reason to learn more.

Hayden was fascinated by this durable, fast-growing plant when he learned it could be used to build everything from skateboards to wood floors. He noticed that each fall, bamboo plants stopped growing when the days grew shorter. The leaves on the plants turned from emerald green to yellow to brown, and then the giant stalks were chopped down to the ground. Hayden was curious about how, in one season, a bamboo plant can grow 7.6 meters (25 feet) in Salt Lake City. Salt Lake City weather can be unpredictable in the spring. Ninety-degree days one week can be followed by snowy days the next. These swings in temperatures can affect how fast plants grow. Thinking about these patterns of growth helped Hayden come up with question he could test scientifically: How do changes in temperature affect daily growth of a bamboo plant in Salt Lake City?

Engineering Projects

Engineers and inventors are responsible for the innovations that power human life. From luxury items such as automatic ice makers and electric toothbrushes to automobiles and airplanes, engineers take an unbelievable idea and make it into reality. Science fair judges like originality, but they also like devices that serve a need or have a real purpose.

The Vitamin C Caper

Jenny Suo and Anna Devathasan of New Zealand decided to study vitamin C levels in different juice drinks. They weren't out to prove anything special. They were just interested in doing a chemistry project for the school science fair. But what they learned ended up costing one company over $160,000 in a lawsuit for false advertising.

Advertisements claimed that the black currants used to make a popular juice drink, Ribena, had four times more vitamin C than oranges. This claim was the *observation* that started their chemistry project. Anna and Jenny read labels and studied advertisements. Their *background research* helped them come up with a *hypothesis* that could be tested using the scientific method. Based on advertised claims about vitamin C, the team *hypothesized that Ribena would have more vitamin C than other juice drinks.*

Scientists already know how to measure vitamin C content. Jenny and Anna selected other juices for testing and outlined the chemicals, equipment, and procedures they would use in the experimental design section of their research plan.

In the end, the 14-year-old scientists came up with some unexpected results: Ribena had *less* vitamin C than orange juice. The false advertising claims were eventually corrected and Ribena drinkers everywhere now know how much of their daily vitamin C intake is coming from this black currant drink.

Robotic Window Washer for Glass Buildings

DANIEL BLAKEMORE (TENTH GRADE)

Second Place, Engineering, Electrical and Mechanical, 2006 Regional Science and Engineering Fair, Salt Lake City.

Daniel Blakemore has been inventing, engineering, and building since he was old enough to play with Lego building blocks. For some time, he had been thinking about how expensive, difficult, and dangerous washing the windows of a tall building must be. A robotic window washer could save money and lives.

FROM INSPIRATION TO DESIGN

To learn more about how existing technology can be repurposed or used in the construction of something new, Daniel subscribes to *Make* magazine. The magazine has opened Daniel's mind to all sorts of new possibilities. One day, while printing something on his home printer, Daniel watched the deliberate movements of the ink jet printer from side to side and then down the page. This *observation* started Daniel thinking that he could use this mechanism to operate the robotic window washer he was designing for the school science fair.

BUILDING, TESTING, AND REFINING PROTOTYPES

Professional engineers and student engineers follow the same basic strategy when they design, build, and test a new device. In the commercial world, companies create and test multiple prototypes before a final product is sold to the public. The most determined science fair students do the same. Getting something to work the way you want it to and finding just the right materials takes time. For Daniel, the process meant he developed new and improved prototypes each year he participated in the science fair, a multi-year project.

Daniel's first robotic window washer, the "Robotic Window Washer for Glass Buildings," used readily available materials that included thousands of Lego blocks. The blocks kept the device from becoming too heavy to attach to a window. Daniel's prototype let him test how well machinery from an inkjet printer worked in moving the window washer from side to side and down the window. This first prototype revealed some real challenges. A robotic window washer had to carry a lot of water, which is heavy, and the robot needed to provide a drip- and streak-free finish. Daniel tackled these challenges in the redesign and construction of additional prototypes.

Engineering Projects: Design Goal and Purpose

The research plan for an engineering project focuses on defining the purpose and goal of the device. Daniel's success came from understanding that engineering projects should always begin by learning what was

Daniel makes some final adjustments to his "Robotic Window Washer for Glass Buildings" before judging at a 2007 regional science and engineering fair.

done before and how it was done. This knowledge can save an engineer time and resources. According to Daniel,

> Background knowledge is a crucial part of any engineering project. Not only does it allow the student to assess how realistic an idea is, but it also lets you see what to do and what not to do based on similar engineering efforts. It may even provide information about aspects of the project or design goal that you didn't know existed.

Profiles in Science Fair Success: Three Top Student Scientists

What if your research could help the government, the people of your community, or the environment? What if you could make a scientific contribution that captured the attention of the media and politicians? What if you could have an experience that helped you set important educational and career goals?

Student scientists have made amazing contributions to society. Many young scientists have an experience that helps define their interests and their college and career plans.

Like creating a great piece of art or building a beautiful home, conducting a great science project doesn't happen overnight. The projects and students in this section can be considered the "Olympic athletes" of science fairs. Read about how inspiration and hard work took three top student scientists on a journey that provided opportunities they never imagined possible.

SIYA XUZA: AN AFFORDABLE, ENVIRONMENTALLY FRIENDLY ROCKET FUEL

I became interested in rockets after a friend suggested the hobby and after watching the movie October Sky about Homer Hickam.

—Siya Xuza

In 2005, the South African Department of Science and Technology announced plans to create a South African Space Agency. It was perfect timing for Siyabulela Xuza (or Siya), a young rocket scientist from the small town of Umtata, South Africa. The announcement reignited Siya's interest in a project he had been working on for four years. At seventeen years old, he would refocus his efforts on creating an affordable, safe, and environmentally friendly rocket fuel. As a developing country, South Africa would need an inexpensive fuel in its quest for space.

Siya's fascination with rockets propelled him thousands of miles from his home in South Africa to the 2007 Intel International Science and Engineering Fair in New Mexico. He received the top two awards in Transportation and Energy for his project, "African Space: Fueling Africa's Quest to Space." Siya Xuza is a 21st-century "rocket boy;" his enthusiasm,

Siya Xuza prepares for a launch. He has built and launched more than ten rockets. This rocket was launched in a field in Meyerton, South Africa. It reached 875 meters (2,781 feet).

intelligence, and work ethic may help move his nation into space. Siya's national pride and hopes for South Africa and the African continent inspired not only his interest in rocketry but also his desire to see more South African youth recognize their potential and become young scientists. Siya hopes his new fuel will become part of a South African space program.

Get a feel for Siya's frustration, determination, and excitement by reading passages from his own research notes on page 27.

ERICA DAVID: SNOW FENCE CONTROLS SNOWDRIFTS IN WYOMING

Erica David lives in the remote Wyoming farming community of Pinedale. The population is 1,400. Her daily routine involves caring for over 100 animals, including sheep, goats, pigs, and horses. In the sixth grade, Erica was looking for a science fair project idea. She started by searching for information about snow, and snow fences captured her attention. Wyoming is famous for heavy snowfalls and high winds. This turbulent weather leads to impressive snowdrifts, when wind-blown snow piles up in inconvenient places. These drifts are troublesome for travelers, farmers, and wild animals alike.

Snow fences are a common fixture across the Wyoming landscape. They are built to control the drifting snow. After seven years of studying ways to build better snow fences, Erica David has become a

In His Own Words

—Siya Xuza

2003

I started building and launching rockets during my school holidays. I was 14 when my very first rocket was ready to fly! After a nerve-wrecking countdown, I pressed the launch button… bang! The rocket exploded on the launch pad! This was my first letdown, and it motivated me to improve my design in order to have a successful flight. After spending a year getting tips from the South African Amateur Rocketry Association, I succeeded. I launched a rocket and it soared to just over 1,000 feet. This was a euphoric moment for me, as it showed the power of perseverance.

2006

The rocket flew to just under 3,000 feet during the flight test and was recovered with no damage. Thus, a small-scale rocket launch was successfully conducted and the experiment proved the fuel could be used on a larger scale for launching low-Earth orbit satellites.

local expert on the topic. She is fondly referred to as the "snow fence girl." Her project was started to find new ways to protect her own farm animals.

Erica David started her work in middle school. The project grew from there. She has demonstrated that whether you are from a small town or a big city, doing student research can be a meaningful learning experience. In 2008, when Erica was a senior in high school, she began working with EnCana Oil and Gas. The company contacted the "snow fence girl" to help design snow fences to protect the migratory routes of pronghorn antelope.

Erica David walks along a snow fence on her farm. Erica designed, developed, and tested this snow fence and has filed for a patent with the U.S. Patent Office. *Inset:* To build better snow fences, Erica tested the temperature and moisture content of snow.

Erica has won numerous awards and scholarships in regional, national, and international science competitions. It is not surprising that this young scientist plans to pursue an environmental engineering degree and wants to continue doing research.

Erica believes in the student research experience. She enjoys helping other aspiring young scientists navigate the world of science fairs or start their own snow science project.

> I live in a very rural community. My backyard clothesline and garage provided my first research site. Anybody can do a science project. You don't have to have the support of a local university or scientists to be successful.
>
> —Erica David

SHANNON BABB: TROUBLED WATERS

In 2006, Shannon Babb was recognized as one of the top student scientists in the country. She won the prestigious Intel Science Talent Search (STS) for her study, "Troubled Waters: A Six-Month Longitudinal Water Quality Study of the Spanish Fork River Drainage System." Her experience as a student scientist rewarded her with more than $200,000 in scholarships and a trip to the Nobel prize ceremonies in Stockholm, Sweden. She presented her research at a congressional reception in Washington, D.C., and met the President of the United States. Her passion for the environment and science shines as she describes the Utah rivers she had studied as "her rivers." Her interest in the well-being of Utah river ecosystems goes far beyond pursuing success in science fairs.

Shannon's research spanned five years, thousands of study samples, and several cold snowy days of water collection and testing. Her efforts focused on studying

Working in the field, Shannon Babb determines phosphorus levels in a water sample.

water quality in the inlets and outlets of Utah Lake. Understanding pollution and "listening to the rivers" became a passion. During her first few years of research, she used babysitting money to pay for some of her test kits; other supplies and equipment were provided by the Utah Stream Team and the Monte L. Bean Museum of Natural History.

"If everyone can look to solve a problem in their own backyard, we could clean up the world," Shannon says. Shannon identified the causes of pollution along the Spanish Fork River drainage system and created a detailed plan to reverse the damage. Her plan included an educational outreach program to teach the public the importance of protecting local waterways. Her passion and dedication made Shannon stand out at numerous national and international science competitions. Her research carries a strong message of concern and a persuasive call for action. This project is a powerful example of what a student can accomplish in her own "backyard."

Some Words From Shannon . . .

ON HER PASSION FOR STUDYING WATER

Thousands of people die each year because of contaminated water. More children die from diarrhea caused by contaminated water than from any other disease. We need water for life. It affects the environment and it affects our health. Understanding, monitoring, and protecting water

Shannon shares her research with members of the Central Valley Water Reclamation Facility and Utah Water Quality Board.

quality [are among] the most important issues facing human beings.

ON HER INSPIRATION TO STUDY RIVER WATER IN HER COMMUNITY

I started thinking about the drought and pollution problems plaguing Utah Lake when I saw a story in the news. Every one of my science fair projects, since eighth grade, has focused on tracking down individual problems that were *causing pollution in Utah Lake. Each year my studies built on the information and discoveries from the previous year.*

HER ADVICE FOR STUDENTS WHO ARE STARTING A RESEARCH PROJECT

Do lots of background research before you get started. The more you do ahead of time, the less you'll have to redesign or repeat experiments. It helps you determine where the resources are and how much data is needed to make your study valid.

Are You Interested in Testing Water Quality?

Shannon's procedures were not new, but investigating water pollution in the rivers she chose was. Shannon learned about these testing procedures in a laboratory field book written for middle school teachers. The testing methods she used are the same as those that professional scientists and environmental monitoring agencies employ.

Find out about the scientific equipment available at your school.
An electromyogram (EMG) can be used to study muscle force during a
variety of activities.

Excavating for Experimental Ideas

How do you find an idea that will inspire you to be a real scientist? Start by thinking about what problems interest you. Maybe you're tired of throwing the ball over and over for your dog to fetch. In 2006, one science fair team at the Intel International Science and Engineering Fair presented a solution to this problem. Creative and original, this solution involved constructing a magnetic ball and dog collar. Fetching canines were successfully entertained by a ball that drifted away each time the dog approached. (Read more about this project in Chapter 8.)

Get Project Ideas From Your Interests

What are your interests and what do you really enjoy doing? Sports, games, or art? How about pets, music, or the environment? Some ideas for converting your interests into science project ideas are brainstorming with teachers, scientists, or family members; tuning into science programs on the television, radio, and Internet; searching the Internet to find out about science research related to your interests; visiting a museum or the visitors' center at a state or national park; reading books on a favorite subject.

Table 3.1 lists some real student projects that developed from unique interests and curiosities.

Brainstorming in Action

How do you convert your interests into a testable research question? The following is a brainstorming exchange led by a science teacher who helped a tenth-grade research team find the right idea for their project, "Reading With Your Senses."

Science Teacher: List some of the things that you find most interesting and fun.

Student Scientists: Kids, reading, art, psychology.

Science Teacher: Would you like to do a project that involves kids and learning?

Student Scientists: Yes.

Science Teacher: Learning and psychology are a great combination. Understanding how kids learn is very important to teachers, parents, schools, and textbook authors. What are some of the most important things children need to learn in elementary school?

Student Scientists: Reading, writing, and math.

TABLE 3.1

Example Projects That Developed Around Student Interests

INTEREST	QUESTIONS AND IDEAS
SHOPPING	Are teen shoppers stereotyped by store employees based on dress (examples: punk, prep, goth)? Does appearance affect how teens are treated in stores?
COMPUTERS	Create an automatic assignment and test reminder. The program will constantly review the class calendar and send e-mail reminders about upcoming tests and assignments.
CATS	Research shows 85 percent of cats, worldwide, are sensitive to catnip. Will 85 percent of the local domestic cats tested respond to catnip?
MUMMIFICATION	What's the best way to mummify a store chicken? Are there better methods than those used by the Egyptians?
POLLUTION	Do coal-burning fire plants cause acidification of nearby snow?
CELL PHONES	Are high school students becoming addicted to text messaging?
FAMILY SIZE	How does birth order affect personality in a large family?
BICYCLE SAFETY	Create a bicycle-to-automobile communication system that will warn automobile drivers when bicyclists are nearby.
FITNESS	How does lung capacity compare for wind instrument players and athletes?

Science Teacher: Teachers use many tools to help students learn to read. They also want to be sure students comprehend and remember what they are reading. Can you think of ways to help students learn to read?

Student Scientists: Acting out a book and using real objects from the story might make the book more fun and easier to remember. You could also use props and sounds to make the story come to life.

Science Teacher: What would you test if you wanted to explore this idea? You need to define a question and a hypothesis to create an experiment. It sounds like you are adding more senses to the reading experience.

There are five senses: sight, sound, touch, smell, and taste. Does this give you any ideas?

Student Scientists: Maybe reading a story and adding things the students can feel (sense of touch), smell, taste, and hear will help the brain focus and remember the story better. It would probably also make reading time more fun.

Can we test the value of adding sensory input to help elementary school children learn to read?

Science Teacher: That's a good idea. You will need ways to measure the effect of different types of sensory input on reading comprehension and recall, age-appropriate reading materials, and permission to run experiments in an elementary school classroom. I think you should design an experiment that will add to the education of the children. Teachers have a busy schedule, and they will not want to lose class time to an activity that could take away from daily learning.

Learn about how this idea was developed into a research plan in Chapter 4.

Inspiration—By Chance!

Give yourself an opportunity to be inspired by opening your eyes to science. Once you begin experimenting, be prepared for the next *inspiration*. It might even be unexpected!

- In the 1940s, Alexander Fleming found that bacterial colonies he was growing and studying were contaminated with a fungus. When he took a closer look he observed that the fungus was killing the bacteria. This discovery led to one of the most important advances in medicine ever—antibiotics. Today, millions of people survive life-threatening illness because of antibiotics!

- Luigi Galvani was an Italian scientist who studied anatomy in the late 1700s. During one study, Galvani suspended frog legs from a wire. By chance, a gust of wind connected the wire to some electrically charged metal. This brief connection sent a pulse of electricity running through the frog legs. The frog legs began moving. This *chance observation* was the first demonstration that electrical currents power muscles inside the body. Today, scientists continue to study electrical connections in the bodies of living things. This field of science is known as neurophysiology.

Chance favors the prepared mind.
—Louis Pasteur

CHAPTER 4

•••••••••••••••••••••

The Research Plan and the Scientific Method

Planning is one of the most important steps in the research process. Planning is also important in our everyday lives. Imagine planning a camping trip. To have a safe and fun trip, you need food, camping equipment, campsite reservations, maps, weather information, first-aid items, and a car with a full tank of gas.

A great research project also involves planning and attention to details. Furthermore, a *research plan* is required to enter most middle and high school science fairs. Even some elementary school teachers ask for a basic research plan. Planning your research will help you produce more meaningful results and a better outcome. Let's take a look at the research plan for the project "Reading With Your Senses" (see Figure 4.1).

The students doing this project had a few special considerations.

- They had to create testing materials appropriate for second-grade students who had only just begun to read.

FIGURE 4.1

Research Plan

Category: Behavioral and Social Sciences
"Reading With Your Senses"
Katie Christilaw and April Buckway (Tenth grade)

Hypothesis: By increasing their sensory experience during the reading of a book, students will achieve improved memory and recall. Memory scores for reading alone will be lower than the scores for reading with added sound, smell, and touch. Students' scores will increase with each type of sensory input added to the reading of a book.

Methods: Subjects: One second-grade class (27 children/ages seven and eight) from a nearby elementary school.

Test three books from the same author (Lynley Dodd). The books are from England and not familiar to the students we will be testing. All books will be read by the same person. Reading comprehension and recall will be tested using a questionnaire. The questionnaire will be short and simple to understand. It will use simple phrases and pictures. The teacher and research team will assist students who need help understanding any of the questions.

Day 1: A children's book will be read to students in Mrs. Stephens's class. Book 1: *Hairy Maclary's Rumpus at the Vet.*
The book will be presented to students sitting in a semicircle to duplicate the normal group-reading experience.

Day 2: We will return to test recall about the book that was read on Day 1. New reading, Book 2: *Slinky Malinki.* Students will again be seated on the floor in a semicircle. The sense of sight will be removed by blindfolding the children. Additional sensory input will come from sound, smell, and touch. My partner and I will bring props to add sensory information as the story is told.

Day 3: Give questionnaire to test reading and comprehension of the book from Day 2. New reading, Book 3: *Hairy Maclary and Zachary Quack.* This time students will not be blindfolded. Sight, sound, feel, and touch will be part of the reading experience.

Day 4: Questionnaire for the book presented on Day 3.
Detailed information about the research project, books, and questionnaires will be given to the principal, teacher, and parents of students involved. Students who do not have parental consent will not be allowed to participate.

Due to potential problems with allergies, the sense of taste will not be included in this study.
**Student identity/names will not be part of any questionnaire/data collected. In order to evaluate potential differences in the responses of girls and boys, we will only ask for information on a student's gender.*

- They needed approval from a safety committee, the elementary school principal, the second-grade teacher, and the parents of the second-grade subjects.

Research plans also include copies or descriptions of testing materials. In this case, parents and teachers would want to know as much as possible about the project. Figure 4.2 is a sample of one of the questionnaires used in "Reading With Your Senses."

Improving the Research Plan

Can you think of ways to improve the research plan for "Reading With Your Senses?" High school scientists often choose to stick with a project for several years, adding more subjects and improving the experimental

FIGURE 4.2

Sample Subject Questionnaire

Reading With Your Senses: Book 3

I am a   Girl   Boy

Instructions: *circle one answer for each question*

1- Have you read this book before?   YES   or   NO

2- Where was Hairy Maclary in this story?

-Pet shop   -Outdoors   -School   -Home   -Store

3- What small animal was Zachary?

4- Do you think that Hairy Maclary and Zachary became friends?

     -Yes   -No   -I can't remember

5- What was **Not** one of the things that you smelled, touched, or felt?

     -A flower   -A spray of water

     -A tree branch   -A strawberry

6- How did Hairy Maclary feel at the end of the story?

Very sad   Happy   Angry   Silly

design with each subsequent project. "Reading With Your Senses" is a well-designed experiment, but a few improvements could be considered.

The books were selected for two reasons:

- The books are written by an English author and unfamiliar to most American children.
- The books have the same writing style and format, making them ideal for testing over multiple days.

Selecting a series may present a problem. Could the children get better at taking the tests? This is a concern because the children are likely to become familiar with the characters, stories, and writing style of the books each day a new one is read and tested.

A possible solution is to add a fourth book on Day 4. By adding this control, the student scientists could learn if the children's test scores were improving as they became more familiar with the author's books. The fourth book should be read to the children using the same procedures followed for the Day 1 control, reading with children seated in a semicircle with no added sights, sounds, smells, or touches. The test results from the Day 1 control story could also be compared to test results on Day 4. If the children did not become more familiar with the story and testing strategy, you would expect to find no differences in the average scores for Day 1 and Day 4.

The research team creates a full sensory reading experience for a second grade classroom. The girl dressed in black acts out the role of Hairy Maclary and uses props to create sounds and smells that follow the story.

Your Own Research Plan

Are you planning to run experiments or design, construct, and test a new device? Once you have made this important decision you will need to plan the project. Table 4.1 summarizes what you need to do to create a research plan for an experimental or engineering project. Planning your project will probably take more time

> The **scientific method** is more than a series of steps. Before getting to work on your research plan, carefully review the experimental examples and steps in the scientific method (later in this chapter).

than you think, but great experiments are always well planned. Think about it. Even when you make cookies, precision produces the best results. And there is no need to try to invent a brand-new recipe for chocolate chip cookies because a lot can be learned from the recipes that already exist.

What Should You Read?

A literature review involves looking for information about the research or engineering project that you are planning. After reviewing published books, science journals, and online databases that contain information

TABLE 4.1

Overview: Creating a Research Plan

EXPERIMENTAL RESEARCH	ENGINEERING PROJECTS
What hypothesis will be tested?	What is the engineering goal, purpose, and need for the device?
Read what is already known about the topic. Use the information to come up with ideas for experiments.	**Read** about similar designs and ideas. Use the information to come up with construction ideas.
Design experiments to test your hypothesis. Outline information about the procedures, materials, and experimental and control groups.	**Design** the device in simple line drawings. Label the parts and list materials. Explain how the device will be built.

on your topic, you will be better informed about what is known and unknown. This information can be used to plan experiments or construction efforts.

Find at least five references. Whenever possible, student scientists should consider interviewing an expert. Experts may be engineers, doctors, scientists, animal-care specialists, dog trainers, mechanics, and others.

> **TIP:** A well-written literature review can be used in the introduction section of your research report and on the poster board. Get it done early and you will have more time to spend on experiments later.

Use these strategies when creating a literature review:

- Read, collect, and photocopy important references.
- Read about what has been done before and how it was done. Highlight the most important information.
- Create a reference page citing the best references and keep adding new references as you find them.

Some samples of reputable references include printed resources, such as:

- current textbooks and encyclopedias
- newspaper articles
- science and news magazines, such as *Time*, *Newsweek*, *Discover*, *Science News Daily*, *Science News for Kids*, *Popular Mechanics*, *Make*, and *Scientific American*
- online resources, such as Centers for Disease Control (CDC), American Cancer Society, and the Environmental Protection Agency

FIGURE 4.3

Sample Literature Review

Select Paragraphs from the
Review of Literature
for "Is Precipitation
Pickling the Environment?"

Breanne Anderson (Grade 10)

Coal-fired power plants account for 96 percent of sulfur oxide and 93 percent of nitric oxide emissions into the air (Sierra Club, 2006). Sulfur oxides and nitric oxides are dangerous to human health, contributing to lung disease and other respiratory problems (McBride, 1978). It has been suggested that cutting coal-fired power plant pollutants by 75 percent would prevent more than 18,000 deaths a year (Sierra Club, 2006). Air pollutants may account for at least 5 percent of hospital admissions (Schwartz, 1999).

Acid precipitation, caused by emissions from coal-fired power plants can destroy ecosystems by disturbing balances in pH, making them unable to support life (Sierra Club, 2006). There are many instances in which acid rain has fallen into a lake causing a drop in normal pH levels, leading to the demise of the fish population and aquatic life. Fish fail to spawn and struggle to find food when pH levels drop to below 4.5 (Bush, 2000).

References

Bush, Mark B. 2000. *Ecology of a changing planet* (2nd Edition), Boston: Prentice Hall.

McBride, J.P., Moore, R.E., Witherspoon, R.E. 1978. http://www.ornl.gov/info/ornlreview/rev2634/text/colmain.html.

Schwartz, Joel. 1999. Air pollution and hospital admissions for heart disease in eight U.S. counties. *Epidemiology*, 10 (1): 17–22.

Sierra Club. 2006. http://www.sierraclub.org/cleanair/factsheets/power.asp.

Refer to Appendix 1 to learn how to run keyword searches using search engines. The appendix also contains a list of Internet addresses for reliable online references.

When you've finished the literature review, summarize facts and information from each reference. A good literature review is the foundation of the introduction section in your final report. Figure 4.3 is a passage taken from a literature review for a high school project

Coal-fired power plants release fine particles into the air and contribute to acid rain. Breanne Anderson, 2006 International Science and Engineering Fair finalist, studied coal particles and the pH of snow downwind from this Wyoming power plant.

that studied the pH of snow around a coal-fired power plants. The review information was later incorporated into the introduction of the final report and poster.

Learn more about writing a research report and formatting a reference list in Chapter 8.

Experiments and the Scientific Method

The scientific method is always easier to understand through examples. Not every question can be answered using the scientific method. Think about defining a testable question and hypothesis by reading the examples that follow.

Experiments begin by asking a question. Once you have your question, propose a *hypothesis*, which is a reasonable answer to the question. Remember, both the question and hypothesis must be testable through experimentation.

Testable: How do humans locate the source of a sound?

Hypothesis: Humans use two ears to locate the source of a sound accurately.

Testable: Do males remember faces better than females?

Hypothesis: Males will remember faces better than females when black-and-white photographs of faces are used in a short-term memory test.

Not testable: Are dogs happy when you feed them steak?

Problem: How do you define or measure "happy" in a dog?

The process of designing experiments to test a hypothesis is called the *scientific method*. In research, experimental results sometimes support the hypothesis and sometimes do not. When one hypothesis or set of experiments doesn't seem to answer the question, scientists go back to the drawing board. They either change the experiments or come up with a new hypothesis to test. Read more about the steps in the scientific method in Table 4.2.

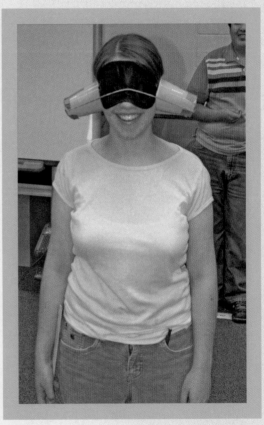

Planning an Engineering Project

Engineering projects don't necessarily involve the scientific method. Engineers build things, so the only time they might think

Be creative when designing experiments. In this class activity, test subjects were fitted with blindfolds, and one, two, or no ear cups. Toy clickers were used to create sound, and test subjects pointed to the sound source using a yardstick.

TABLE 4.2

The Scientific Method: Planning Experimental Research

SCIENTIFIC METHOD	THE RULES AND STEPS IN THE SCIENTIFIC METHOD
MAKE OBSERVATIONS	Use your senses—sight, hearing, smell, touch, taste—or an extension of your senses: microscope, thermometer, tape recorder, camera
ASK A QUESTION	The question reveals what you would like to know. The question must be testable through experimentation.
FORMULATE A HYPOTHESIS	A scientific guess to answer the question. The hypothesis must be testable through experimentation.
DESIGN EXPERIMENTS	Experimental studies include control and experimental group(s). Experiments must be repeatable. Control group—Helps identify experimental effects. Serves as a basis for comparison. *Control groups are important for making sure the results (data) were not created by chance or caused by how the experiment was done.* Experimental group(s)—Provides the data that either support or refute the hypothesis. To test a hypothesis, change only one experimental variable at a time. Example: Hypothesis—*Plants need light to grow.* Control group—*Five plants grown in the dark.* Experimental group—*Five plants grown with light.* All other variables are kept the same between the two groups. *Plants are the same type and age, grown with the same brand of fertilizer and soil. They all receive the same amount of water, and grow in rooms at the same temperature.*

about using the scientific method is when testing the new device. So it's not surprising that young engineers need to follow a different set of steps when they are planning a project (Figure 4.4).

Some of the greatest engineering innovations are very simple. In 2007 a team of high school scientists was looking for an engineering idea with an environmental benefit. They focused on ways to reduce carbon dioxide emissions. Their idea used existing technology and materials to create something new.

An Extraordinary Light

Think about all of the lights in your house. In most cities, turning on a light requires a coal-fired power plant to provide the energy, but that plant causes pollution. What if light energy could be used for more than just illuminating a room? Less wasted energy would mean less pollution. This was the thought process behind designing an extraordinary light. The students did *background research* to learn about how coal-fired power plants contribute to global warming. They also read about solar cells (photovoltaic cells) and rechargeable batteries. The team took a standard lamp and modified it to include solar cells and a battery charger. Then, each time the lamp was switched on, solar cells captured energy from the light bulb, which then charged the battery. No more plugging rechargeable

FIGURE 4.4

Basic Steps in an Engineering Project

Come up with an **idea for a device.**

Write a **design goal.**
What is the purpose/function of the device?

Construction plans
Create a materials list, diagrams, and instructions for constructing the device. The original plan may change and be improved once construction begins.

Build
Assemble the device according to the design plans.

Test the prototype device to see if and how well it works. Make improvements and retest.

batteries into the wall where they would refill with energy from coal burning somewhere in the distance.

With an idea and some background research, this team of scientists planned their project. Figure 4.5 shows their research plan.

The research plan might be the most important part of the research process, although, too often, students want to start experimenting or engineering so badly they neglect this important first step. Reading the literature before starting a project and writing a detailed research plan will always produce the best results.

Once you have a research plan, manage your project by scheduling deadlines and setting goals. If you are realistic and stick to the deadlines, you will finish your project before the science fair without ever losing a night's sleep. Research projects can be divided into stages. See page 60 to learn more about creating a timeline for your own project.

Three high school engineers designed this device that floats on top of salt water and uses magnets and electricity to move under the direction of the sun. The project was awarded third place in the team category at the Intel International Science and Engineering Fair.

Research Equipment

Science is definitely more fun when you let your imagination run wild, but sometimes resources limit what you can do. Think about what you'll need to run experiments or to engineer a device before spending too much time writing the research plan. Perhaps you will find ways to build the testing equipment or repurpose things from your home to get the project done. Sometimes you will need to borrow or buy your own equipment. Here are some ideas for finding the resources you may need:

- Contact laboratories at a local college or university.
- Borrow equipment, such as stethoscopes and blood pressure cuffs, from a local hospital or clinic. And ask the facility if they can donate used equipment to your school.
- Under adult supervision, look for secondhand equipment online.
- Contact a local museum.
- Ask your science teachers what resources are available through your school.

Educational grade laboratory equipment is available through science supply companies (see Appendix 2). This equipment is affordable and portable. And it is used by schools across the country. Vernier Software and Technology provides high-tech testing devices designed for student use. Vernier also sells lab manuals and features free, innovative project ideas on their

FIGURE 4.5

Research Plan

Category: Engineering

"An Extraordinary Light"

Chris Arita and Mike Adamson (Twelfth Grade)

Design Goal: Build a lamp that has small solar panels attached to the underside of a lampshade. Wire the solar panels to a rechargeable battery system. Light energy will be captured and used to charge batteries.

Purpose: Capturing light energy from household lamps is an energy-efficient way to charge batteries. Wide-scale use could lower carbon dioxide emissions and reduce manufacturing of new batteries.

Materials: Lamp with shade from a secondhand store: The lamp stem will have a hollow core and base to hide wires running from the battery charger to the solar panels; solar cells (photovoltaic cells): 2" × 1" with wiring already attached; rechargeable battery and charge base; 100-watt tungsten light bulb; multimeter to measure charge.

Construction: [Note: A well-labeled diagram should always be created. (Hand-drawn images work great.)] *Lamp:* Measure lamp height and diameter of lampshade. Provide details on the placement of solar cells and wiring. *Wiring:* Diagram how the solar cells will be wired through the lamp to the base where the batteries will be charged.

Testing: Before testing the device, check that solar cells are working and can receive energy.

Preparing batteries: Drain several new rechargeable batteries by using them to power a flashlight until the light goes out.

Capturing wasted light/energy: Turn lamp on and every 10 minutes use a multimeter to measure the charge available in the battery.

Date Analysis: Graph the rate that the battery is charged from lamp light and solar cells.

Web site. *Remember, you can have an original question and then use methods that are already available to design experiments and find answers.*

Here's a sample of some of the tools available to student scientists: electrocardiogram sensors for measuring heart activity (EKG), grip-strength testing (dynamometer), soil-testing probes, barometers, radiation detectors, force sensors (good for testing force and motion on roller coasters), and more. Just think about the questions, hypotheses, and experiments that can be done with this equipment.

Create a Timeline to Manage Your Project

Start by dividing your project into phases. Then, add specific goals and deadlines for each phase of the research process. Most projects can be divided into six phases:

1. Write a research plan. Design experiments or create engineering plans.
2. Learn about science competitions, including rules and entry requirements.
3. Work on experiments or construct the device. Keep careful records in a project notebook.
4. Analyze and interpret results from experiments. Test the engineering prototype and analyze results.
5. Write a report and display information in a scientific poster.
6. Practice for the science fair.

●●●●●●●●●●●●●●●●●

The Rules: Safety, Originality, and Consent

Before beginning any experimental or engineering project, student scientists need to understand contest rules. School science fairs don't usually have a lot of rules and paperwork, but that's not true for most state and national science competitions. For example, some science contests may not allow projects on human or animal behavior. Also, students who engineer and test a new device should expect limitations and strict safety guidelines if their project involves working with fuels or other explosives. Begin the research process by considering contest rules.

Most science competitions publish rules and information online. A list of science competitions can be found in Chapter 10.

If You Don't Follow the Rules

Several years ago, at a state science fair, one grand prize winner was disqualified from advancing to the Intel International Science and Engineering Fair (ISEF). The project studied and compared bacterial levels in the men's and women's bathrooms at a local school. To study the bacteria, the young scientist converted a bathtub and home bathroom into a mini-laboratory. This is where she cultured (grew) and studied the microorganisms. She was very careful and followed an impressive number of safety precautions that had been provided by a supervising research scientist.

The young scientist was devastated to learn that ISEF rules don't allow students to perform research on bacteria in their homes. This rule does not consider the types of bacteria or the safety measures taken by the student. There are no exceptions. The project was therefore disqualified.

It is critical to know the rules before you start your experiments!

Understanding Science Fair Rules and Guidelines

Science fair rules and safety concerns are broken down into four categories.

SAFETY CONCERNS
- the student scientist
- research animals or human subjects
- greater public
- the environment

ACADEMIC INTEGRITY
- Ensuring a project is *original* and not partly or entirely plagiarized

Experiments involving human subjects require careful planning. This student's project investigated whether diet affects the properties of saliva. Before getting started, a dentist reviewed the research plan and provided safety recommendations. This study involved testing high school subjects, so the student scientist obtained parental consent and worked under the supervision of a science teacher.

CONSENT TO PARTICIPATE IN A SCIENCE COMPETITION

- Students under eighteen years old must have parental consent to enter a science fair outside of their school.

CONSENT FROM HUMAN SUBJECTS

- Human subjects must complete paperwork and provide informed consent. Informed consent means that research subjects have been *informed* about the experiments and the tests in which they will participate. They have provided their *consent* and are willing participants. Research on minors also requires parental consent.

Dealing with contest rules and paperwork can be difficult for students, especially when the science fair is months away and there is no way of knowing how well the project will turn out. Great projects are disqualified each year. Learn the rules and follow them. Don't let your project get disqualified!

Three Steps to Make Sure Your Project Does Not Break Any Rules

1. List the science contests you would like to enter. Ask your science teacher for opportunities in your state and review Chapter 10 to learn about national and international science competitions.
2. Order a rule book or learn about rules and paperwork on the science contest's Web site.
3. Ask a science teacher or mentor to review the contest rules, your research plan, and your paperwork.

Get Informed: Projects That Raise Safety Concerns

Rules and safety guidelines are created to protect research subjects, the student scientist, and the general public. While writing the research plan think about how experiments can be designed safely. Whether you're a student scientist or a professional scientist, research rules and guidelines carry a similar message and purpose.

Think about your project and consider the questions that follow to address safety and science fair rules. If your project fits into one or more of these categories, be sure that you check the rules for any science fairs you want to enter.

ANIMALS
- Where will you find test animals?
- Do the test animals have a backbone? Are they mammals?
- How will the test animals be cared for?
- Will the test animals be subject to any stress or discomfort?
- Are animals an essential part of running the experiment?

HUMAN SUBJECTS
- Will any subjects be under the age of 18?
- Will test subjects be under stress or subject to pain at any time?
- How will subjects' consent be obtained and confidentiality protected?

MICROORGANISMS
- Where are you allowed to study or grow microorganisms?
- Do you need supervision from a scientist or teacher?
- Are there strains or types of organisms that cannot be studied?
- How will you dispose of waste materials? Are there safety guidelines?

ELECTRICITY

- What are the safety guidelines for working with electricity?
- What are the restrictions for demonstrating or displaying a project that uses electricity at a science fair? *Science fair judges like to see how things work. Engineering devices are generally on display and ready for demonstration.*

HAZARDOUS DEVICES OR MATERIALS

Will the project involve working with

- flames, or flammable or explosive materials or devices?
- lasers?

This student extracted caffeine from tea, coffee, and other drinks using a variety of chemicals. Science fair rules required Material Safety Data Sheets (MSDS) on each chemical he used.

- radiation or radioactive materials?
- toxic chemicals?

Safety Committees

Most high school science contests require that projects involving humans, animals, microorganisms, or dangerous chemicals be reviewed by a safety committee.

In student research, scientific committees can be divided into two types: The Institutional Review Board and the Scientific Review Committee. Most regional and state science fairs follow guidelines required by the Intel International Science and Engineering Fair. Learn more about these committees, who serves on them, and how to assemble your own safety committee below.

INSTITUTIONAL REVIEW BOARD (IRB)

An IRB committee protects the safety and privacy of human research subjects. Most regional, national, and international research competitions have their IRB committee.

There are a minimum of three members of an IRB committee including

- science teacher, appropriate to the topic, such as chemistry, biology, geology, or physics;
- school administrator, such as a principal or vice-principal;
- scientific expert, with the knowledge needed to evaluate potential physical or psychological risks, such as registered nurses, medical doctors, psychologists, or physical therapists.

SCIENTIFIC REVIEW COMMITTEE (SRC)

An SRC committee's purpose is to protect the student scientist, test animals, general population, and environment. The key concerns are ensuring the safety of projects involving animal subjects, infectious agents, microorganisms, or hazardous chemicals.

There are a minimum of three members of an SRC committee, including

- biomedical scientist such as a medical doctor, veterinarian, dentist, or research scientist (Ph.D.);
- science teacher appropriate to the topic;
- additional scientist or other professional who is knowledgeable about the research topic and capable of evaluating the safety of the project.

When Will the Project Be Reviewed?

In high school research, most contests have their own independent IRB and SRC committees. This means that each time the project is entered into a new research contest, new committees review procedures, competition paperwork, and subject consent forms to make sure the project was done safely and according to the rules.

The first IRB or SRC review is organized by the student, a science teacher, or school. If appropriate experts cannot be found, contact your regional or state science fair and ask for help.

CHAPTER 6

THE PROJECT NOTEBOOK: A SCIENTIST'S COOKBOOK

Once you've written a research plan, you're ready to begin experimenting or engineering. Keeping detailed, well-organized records is one of the most important things a scientist must do.

What Is a Project Notebook?

Follow your mom's recipe for your favorite cookies and chances are your cookies will turn out just as good every time you take them. Great scientists keep accurate and detailed notes on their work. They can review their notes at any time and use the information to repeat an old experiment or borrow ideas for a new one. Like great cooks, scientists often share information and exchange ideas. The notes or "recipe" they wrote can allow another scientist to use the same methods to answer a new question.

If you enter a science fair, the judges reviewing your work will want to see your notebook. They'll expect to find your thoughts and data records from the beginning to end. The best way to keep a notebook is to write it like a *journal* or *diary* and date every entry in chronological order.

Journaling for Science

Use a durable notebook. Composition or journaling books that have permanent pages work best. Number the pages and date each entry. Students who decide to use binders should beware. Over time, pages may end up lost, in the wrong order, or damaged. If you have questions or problems along the way, detailed records will allow a mentor scientist or teacher to provide more meaningful help.

These high school students record data from a biology experiment in their project notebook. It is best to use a notebook with permanent pages (inset).

When the research is finished and your poster is ready for the science fair, don't forget your project notebook. Most judges are scientists. They know the value of good records, and they will want to see yours.

A project notebook will be the *record*, *proof*, and *reference* for all of the work you do. (see Table 6.1).

WHAT DETAILS SHOULD YOU INCLUDE IN YOUR NOTEBOOK?

- Keep records of your research project in chronological order and date each entry, just like a diary.
- Write comments to explain what you were doing on a given day. Include successes, failures, and any changes made to the original research plan.
- Tape or glue in photographs (or list digital photo files).
- Write about unexpected, yet important, new discoveries and record these observations in your notebook.

When it is time to write entries in the project notebook some students worry too much about penmanship. Writing in perfect cursive is not important. Keeping thorough records is. Take a moment to consider three mistakes commonly made by student scientists.

WHAT NOT TO DO WITH YOUR NOTEBOOK

- **Don't worry about neatness.** Cross out changes; a simple X is perfect. Never remove any pages. Judges and teachers like to see how the process unfolded. In fact, they like to see the messy notes

TABLE 6.1

TEEN SCIENCE FAIR SOURCEBOOK

What Goes Into a Project Notebook?

EXPERIMENTAL NOTEBOOK	ENGINEERING NOTEBOOK
Copy of the original research plan (see Chapter 4)	Copy of the original engineering plan and construction diagrams (see Chapter 4)
Experiments and procedures	Notes and drawings on construction efforts
Information about materials, methods, observations, problems, data, changes made to the experiment, ideas for future studies, and more.	Hand-drawn diagrams and flow charts to illustrate progress and design changes; materials that were used on a given day; programming code (Copy the code and tape it into your notebook.)
Data recorded into tables (when possible)	Problems and changes in the plans
What do the data mean? Results that support or disprove the original hypothesis	Efforts to test the prototype: data, photographs, video, or other records of testing
Problems encountered during experimentation, including • possible reasons for problems • changes in the methods that could fix problems.	Problems encountered during construction and testing, including • possible reasons for problems • redesign changes used to address problems.
Ideas for future experiments	Ideas for new and improved versions of the device

and changes that show you did the work! Scientific notebooks aren't written for English teachers, and artistic flare won't result in extra points during judging at the science fair.

- **Don't write notes on loose pieces of paper.** They tend to get lost. It is also difficult to put things together in the right order. If you don't happen to have your notebook with you during an experiment, tape, staple or glue loose note pages into the notebook as soon as possible.
- **Never put off writing entries.** It's easiest to record observations and data while the experiments are being done. Later, you are likely to forget important details.

No two notebooks will ever look the same, even if two scientists work on similar projects. The way experimental results, observations, and other details are documented is up to the scientist. A great project notebook has all the information and details needed to repeat the experiments and every bit of data recorded into its pages. In much the same fashion, engineering project notebooks include materials and construction details, as well as meticulous notes on what worked and what didn't.

HOW SHOULD YOU ORGANIZE YOUR PROJECT NOTEBOOK?

Each time a scientist works on a project, the notebook should be at hand. Don't just record data; reflect on what you've learned and how the project is progressing. If need be, the project notebook will help you repeat and improve experiments. It's also a valuable reference for writing your final research report and creating an effective scientific poster.

A well-organized project notebook includes a title page and a table of contents (see Figure 6.1).

FIGURE 6.1

Sample Title Page and Contents From an Organized Project Notebook

Title Page

Scientist Information
Project Title
Student Name, Grade
Teacher Name
School Name, School Address, and School Telephone Number
Caution: Avoid including personal information such as your home address!

If found, please return to the above address or contact my school. Thank you.

Table of Contents

After the title page, leave 2–3 blank pages for the table of contents. Complete this section when the project is finished.
Example:

Pages   1–3   Brainstorming (Ideas for Designing Experiments)
Pages   4–6   Research Plan
Pages   7–35   Experimentation (Experiments in Chronological Order)
Pages 36–47   Data Analysis (Graphs, Statistics, etc.)
Pages 48–52   Discussion of the Data

CHAPTER 7

● ● ● ● ● ● ● ● ● ● ● ● ● ● ● ● ● ● ●

Data Doctor: What to Do With the Numbers

Once you complete your experiment, you may have numbers that need statistical analysis. This chapter will help familiarize you with some statistical tests. But you should ask your science or math teacher to help you determine the most appropriate math tools for analyzing your data. You should also consult a statistics book (see Further Reading).

Why Statistics?

Statistics is a way of making sense out of all the data you have collected. It is also a way of telling other people what your data mean. It's like making numbers tell a story with meaning.

Most experiments will involve a limited number of tests. Research studies may involve experiments on 10–100 dogs, 50–100,000 people, 10–1,000 plants.

For students, the sample size may be limited by time and resources. Bigger samples are generally better, but sometimes you have to work with what you can get. This is where statistics can make a difference. By using statistics you can find meaning in a smaller sample.

Statistical Tools and Terms

Believe it or not, we all think in statistical terms every day. We just don't realize it. At one time or another, virtually every student has negotiated with a parent and "played the odds" to get out of or delay doing homework. You may have asked yourself, "How likely is it that my parents will let me stay out with my friends past 10:00 P.M.?" This question has to do with *probability*, which is at the heart of statistics.

"Is there any connection between doing my homework and being able to go out?" This question asks about the relationship between doing homework and being able to go out. In statistical terms, this is called a *correlation*. Correlations are a type of statistical test.

What Statistics Should You Know?

Middle and high school students have a variety of tools in their mathematical "tool box." These tools can be used to bring meaning to data in a research project.

Middle school scientists may be able to
- calculate an average, mean and mode;
- calculate percentages and work with fractions;
- create and understand bar and line graphs;
- calculate the rate or slope of a line;
- determine probability.

High school students should be able to work with
- standard deviations;

- computer spreadsheet programs (such as Excel) to create tables, charts, and graphs.

Talking Statistics: Learning About the Personality of Numbers

Groups of numbers are like people: They have personalities! Some groups of numbers are very much alike, while other groups of numbers are very different. Consider these descriptions of two people:

LAURA: Laura is a generally happy person, and her mood doesn't change a whole lot. If people were to rank Laura's happiness for the past five days on a scale of 1 to 10 (with 10 being very happy and 5 being average), they would say she was a 5, 5, 5, 5, 5.

MELISSA: Melissa is a bit harder to predict. Depending on the day, she can be either very happy or very sad. If people were to rank Melissa's happiness for the last five days, they would say she was a 1, 9, 4, 2, 9.

HOW CAN LAURA'S AND MELISSA'S HAPPINESS BE DESCRIBED IN STATISTICAL TERMS?

The *mean* will tell us their "average level of happiness." The mean is the average of all scores. Both Laura and Melissa have a mean happiness score of 5.

The *standard deviation* is another statistic. Is it accurate to say Laura and Melissa feel the same level of happiness because they have the same mean level (5) of happiness? Probably not! Melissa's level of happiness varies more than Laura's does. Including *standard deviation* values with a *mean* for a group of numbers is one way to reveal the spread, or differences, in the numbers. For Melissa and Laura, standard deviation values show that these two girls do not actually feel the same level of happiness from day to day. Laura's standard deviation is 0. Melissa's is 3.8.

Tip: Standard deviation values can be calculated, by hand, using the mathematical formula for this function. But it is far easier to let a scientific calculator or spreadsheet program such as Excel do the work.

Graphs

One helpful way to reveal the personality of a group of numbers is to organize them into graphs. Some of the most common statistical graphs are *bar graphs*, *line graphs*, and *scatterplots*. Bar graphs show numerical data as rectangular blocks. The height of the block represents how frequently any score appears in a group. Bar graphs can reveal the true meaning of a group of numbers (or their personality). Bar graphs are useful in comparing average values for different groups or categories.

FIGURE 7.1

A Sample Bar Graph

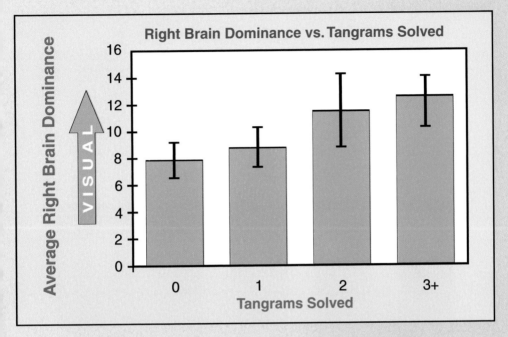

In this example, student scientists used a written test to score right brain dominance in research subjects. The more right brain dominant, the more visual a person is. They then asked the same subjects to solve tangram puzzles during a carefully timed test. In the graph, the average right brain dominance score was compared to success in solving tangrams.

By adding standard deviation values to the bars in this graph, it's easy to see that the only real difference in puzzle solving abilities is between group-0 and group-3+. This suggests that there is a difference in right brain dominance scores for only the best and the worst tangram solvers.

We'll look at line graphs and scatterplots in some later examples, but first let's look at some types of data that can be put into graphs.

Percentages, Frequencies, and Probabilities

Groups of numbers can be broken into smaller pieces. Think of the different candy colors in a bag of M&M's. They are smaller pieces of a large group. In a bag of 100 M&M's, there are the following colors and amounts:

BROWN	13
YELLOW	14
RED	13
BLUE	24
ORANGE	20
GREEN	16

FREQUENCY: *How often or how frequently numbers appear in a given category.*

If you like to eat the blue candies, you're in luck. A typical bag of candies has 24 blue and 20 or fewer of every other color. That means blue candies have a greater frequency than brown or orange or green. Blue candies appear more often or more frequently.

PERCENTAGES: *The proportion of something per 100.*

Percentages tell you how often smaller pieces appear in relation to the whole group. If there are 16 green M&M's out of 100, then 16 percent of the M&M's are green.

PROBABILITY: *A measure of how likely something is.*

Here's the fun part. Once you know the frequency of smaller groups within a larger group, you can start to predict things! How likely are you to pick an orange M&M from a bag of 100 M&M's? You can make predictions using information you already have. For every 100 candies, 20 are orange. If you randomly draw an M&M out of the bag:

- There are 20 chances out of 100 it will be orange.
- 20 percent of the time it will be orange.
- 20/100 or 1 out of 5 candies will be orange.

In statistical terms, the probability or odds of getting an orange M&M is 1 in 5.

Now that you've learned the basic language of statistics, you need to know how to apply it. Among other things, you need to be able to use it to tell other people (and yourself) what your groups of numbers (data) mean. Fortunately, several statistical tests have been designed for just this purpose.

Correlations

A correlation describes how closely two things go together. A correlation is expressed as a number between −1.0 and +1.0, where 0 means absolutely no relationship. This number is called the *correlation coefficient.*

There are two important characteristics of a correlation:

- **Strength:** When two things go together very well, they are said to be strongly correlated. The stronger a correlation is, the closer its coefficient will be to 1.0 or –1.0.

- **Direction:** This refers to how one thing moves in relation to the other.

A *positive* correlation means the two things move in the same direction. In other words, as one goes up, the other goes up, and as one goes down, the other goes down. A perfect positive correlation has a correlation coefficient of 1.0.

A *negative* correlation means the two things move in opposite directions. In other words, as one goes down, the other goes up. A perfect negative correlation has a correlation coefficient of –1.0.

While a correlation describes how well two things go together, it does not say anything about cause and effect. To understand this, think about this *true* example: *There's a positive correlation between ice cream sales and shark attacks.* Does this mean more ice cream sales cause shark attacks? Perhaps sharks like the taste of ice cream? No! Just because two things are related, it does not mean that one causes the other. Can you think of another, more likely explanation for the positive correlation between ice cream sales and shark attacks?

Scatterplots

An easy way to see a correlation is in a graph called a *scatterplot*. To create a scatterplot, plot the scores for one measure on the x-axis and plot the scores that are being compared on the y-axis. Consider the saying,

"When the cat's away, the mice will play." For fun, think about a fake experiment to put this adage to the test.

The experiment:
- 6 rooms with 10 mice in each of them
- Room #1 has 5 cats in it, room #2 has 4 cats, and room #3 has 3 cats, and so on
- In each room, you count the number of mice playing and record the data

To create a *scatterplot* of these data, plot "Number of cats" on the *x*-axis and "Number of mice playing" on the *y*-axis:

By looking at the *scatterplot* for these data, you can tell the strength and direction of the correlation.

- It's a strong correlation. Almost all of the dots fall in a straight line. If all points fell exactly on the line the correlation would be −1.0. (*A line that is*

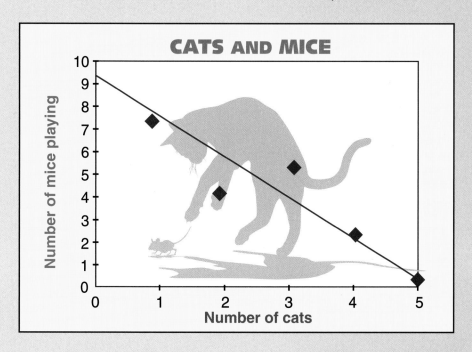

oriented in the opposite direction would be +1.0.) The more random the data points, the weaker the correlation. *This type of graph and calculations of correlations can be accomplished using Excel spreadsheets.*

• The relationship is negative since one measure goes up as the other measure goes down.

• The correlation coefficient for the relationship between mice in the room and number of cats playing is –0.96.

A scatterplot can also be used to make predictions. Draw a straight line that most closely fits all the dots on the scatterplot. This is called a *regression line or best-fit line.* By looking at the line, can you predict how many mice would be playing if 4.5 cats were in the room (ignoring, for a moment, what half a cat would look like!)? How many cats would you expect to be in the room if 6 mice were playing?

Statistical Significance

In research, scientists look for meaningful results. Discovering that your data doesn't produce meaningful results can be disappointing. That is where statistics becomes important. Scientists can sometimes use statistics to find a result that is *statistically significant* even from a small sample.

When data is statistically significant, it means the results were so unusual that it was unlikely they happened by chance alone. Most scientific data will be accepted as statistically significant under one of the following two conditions:

- 95 percent likely the result was not produced by chance or <5 percent likelihood it was a chance occurrence. *This value is p, which can be likened to *probability*. This level of significance would be expressed as $p < 0.05$.
- 99 percent likely the result was not produced by chance or <1 percent likelihood it was a chance occurrence. Data that fit this standard are considered "highly significant," and are expressed as $p < 0.01$.

Chi-Square

Most data can be placed on a numerical scale of some sort. For instance, weight can be measured in kilograms, height can be measured in centimeters, and age can be measured in years. These types of data are called numerical data.

Some data cannot be measured on a scale but can be assigned to a category. Consider gender. Humans are either male or female. In other words, people fall into one of two categories. We call this *categorical data*. Other types of categorical data include hair color, nationality, and political affiliation. One statistical test, specifically designed to use with categorical data is called *chi-square*.

The Three Steps in a Chi-Square Test

1. Make a prediction on how you expect data to sort into the different categories (frequencies).

2. Study a population and determine how the members actually sort into the different categories.

3. Use the chi-square test to compare how the predicted frequencies compare to the frequencies you actually observed.

Chi-square tells you if data don't fit the expected or predicted distribution into categories.

Chi-Square in Action

EXAMPLE 1: Compare "left-footed" and "right-footed" soccer players.

Prediction: I predict 50 percent of soccer players are left-footed while the other 50 percent are right-footed. In other words, 50 out of 100 soccer players are predicted to be left-footed and the other 50 right-footed. This is your *expected frequency*.

Observation: Interview and test 100 soccer players to find out how many are left-footed and how many are right-footed. This will reveal how the population actually sorts into the two categories. This is the *observed frequency*.

Chi-Square: Use chi-square to compare how the *expected frequency* for left- and right-foot preferences compares to the observed frequency for left- and right-foot preference.

Problem: What if a soccer player says he or she can kick equally well with both feet?

Two Options: Do not use that player *or* redo your experiment and add a third category for players who can kick equally well with the left or right foot.

EXAMPLE 2: Do ice cream flavor preferences at my school differ from student flavor preferences nationally? In this example, each ice cream flavor is a category.

Data: Predicted values: Look up statistics on the popularity of flavors among students in the United States.

Observed values: Ask 100 students from my school which types of ice cream they like best.

Results: Record data into a table and then analyze using a chi-square test.

The only thing you can measure here is frequency— that is, how many people like each category of ice cream. For this reason, a chi-square test is the test to use. What will a chi-square test reveal? There are two possibilities:

- The results could show that students from the school have the same taste in ice cream flavors as students nationally. In this case, the result of a chi-square test should be close to 0 (which indicates no difference).

- The results could show that students from the school have different tastes in ice cream flavors compared to students nationally. In this case, the result of a chi-square test should be a number that is not 0.

Let's say the chi-square test for goodness of fit on the actual data produces a result of 20.91. The level of significance for this value can be looked up in a chart. The chart shows that the results are significant, $p < 0.05$. In conclusion, ice cream preferences at this school differ significantly from ice cream preferences for students around the United States.

T-Test (or Student's T-Test)

The most common type of t-test is a t-test for independent means. This test lets you compare results measured from one group to results measured from another group, such as a control group.

EXAMPLE: Americans like to watch television. The following example takes a look at using t-tests in a fictitious science experiment involving TV viewing.

Observation: People watch a lot of TV.

Question: Do people who watch at least ten hours of TV a week read less than people who do not watch TV?

Experiment: Divide ten subjects into two groups of five people each.

Group #1/experimental group: Watches at least ten hours of television a week

Group #2/control group: Watches no television

Data: Each person (Groups 1, 2) is asked to record the amount of time they spend reading every week.

The findings can be recorded in a table.

Analysis: Does the experimental group read less than the control group? To be meaningful, the difference needs to be significant.

When you run a t-test, you find the result is significant at the 5 percent level ($p < .05$). This means that there's less than a 5 percent probability these results occurred by chance. The results are statistically significant.

ANOVA

So far, the tests we have looked at can only be used to compare two sets of data. What do you do if you want to compare *more* than two things? One statistical test that has been designed to compare three or more groups is the *ANOVA* (Analysis of Variance). Be careful. An ANOVA has limitations! It will tell you whether one or more of your groups is significantly different from the other groups. It will not tell you which group or groups it is!

If you want to perform ANOVA, check a statistics book or ask your science teacher, math teacher, or mentor for help.

Getting Help: Mentors

At the 2006 Intel International Science and Engineering Fair, an engineering team shared its invention, a magnetic ball that promised to provide any retrieving dog hours of enjoyment (first introduced in Chapter 3). This imaginative concept captured the attention of many visitors during the public session of the science fair. The device was original and simple but, unfortunately, underdeveloped.

Who could have helped or provided mentorship for this project?
- science teacher
- math teacher
- engineer
- veterinarian
- humane society
- dog trainer

What was this project missing?

THERE WAS NOT ENOUGH TEST DATA; ONLY ONE DOG WAS USED IN TESTING.
- Testing should include a variety of dogs that enjoy retrieving.

- Each dog should be tested several times on different days.
- The average retrieving time for each dog tested could then be plotted in a bar graph: Average retrieving time in minutes versus dogs tested.

THERE WAS ALSO NO VIDEO FOOTAGE FOR THE RETRIEVING TESTS.

This footage could have been created using a digital camera and then displayed on a laptop placed in front of the project poster.

ONLY ONE TYPE OF MAGNETIC BALL AND COLLAR WAS TESTED.

Multiple prototypes could have been created to test ball- and collar-weight as well as ball-texture preferences.

Some other questions that should have been considered are: Is there an optimal ratio for dog size: ball weight and collar weight? Does the weight of the ball affect how long a dog will continue retrieving it?

Finding Help

It is best to seek the advice of an expert when you have a thorough, well-written research or engineering plan. Your plan demonstrates a commitment to the project and lets the expert know you are looking for help and not someone to do the project for you. No matter where you are in the project, when asking an expert for help, always remember to include a copy of the original research plan.

When to Get Help

Mentors and experts can help you in every part of your project:

- **Research plan or engineering plan:** information on work that has been done in the past; methods and tools to use in your project

- **Experimentation or construction of a prototype:** answers to questions; solutions to problems

- **Data analysis:** statistical tests; making graphs; interpreting results

- **Research report:** ways to present findings; how to state valid conclusions

- **Poster display:** best methods for communicating results, trends, and conclusions

- **Judging:** Ideas and strategies for explaining the project and answering questions during judging

- **Moving to another competition:** advice on how to improve and expand the project

Finding the Right Mentor

SCIENCE TEACHERS

School science teachers come from varied backgrounds. Some teachers have worked in industry or have prior research experience. Math teachers can be helpful for figuring out how to graph and test data (statistically).

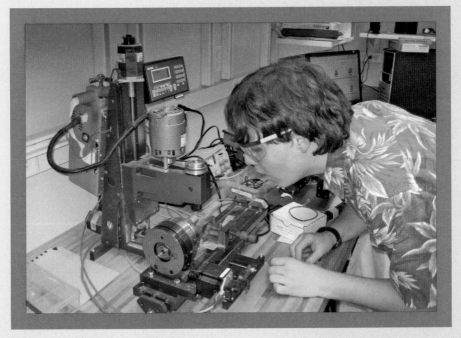

Mentors can provide guidance, access to equipment, and an opportunity to take a project to the next level. This student was able to work with machining equipment in the bioengineering department of a local university.

ENGINEERS

Engineers are mechanically minded innovators. Engineering students from a local college or working engineers are often willing to help. Engineers can be very specialized. For example, a mechanical engineer might provide tips on creating a device that uses gears, whereas a structural engineer might address questions about the strength of a bridge.

RESEARCH SCIENTISTS

Specialized scientists from a university, industry, or research facility are sometimes willing to help young scientists from the community. First decide what type of help you need. Then go to the university Web site and read about faculty members from the appropriate department. (Example: Cell biologists can be found in a biology department.) Contact the departmental office (for example, the biology department) and ask the administrative staff to help you connect with scientists willing to serve as mentors.

MEDICAL PROFESSIONALS

Doctors, nurses, and other health care specialists from local medical facilities can teach students how to measure blood pressure, count pulse, and chart other vital signs. They can also evaluate a research plan and review methods to make sure experiments are safe and well designed.

ANIMAL EXPERTS

A local veterinarian or animal technician understands animal behavior and can offer useful insight into selecting animals for testing. These medical professionals can also review the research plan to make sure experiments are safe for test animals.

Other animal experts include
a) Humane Society: Information about animal behavior and health
b) Dog trainers: Information about behavior and training strategies
c) Veterinarians and other animal-care specialists who work in zoos

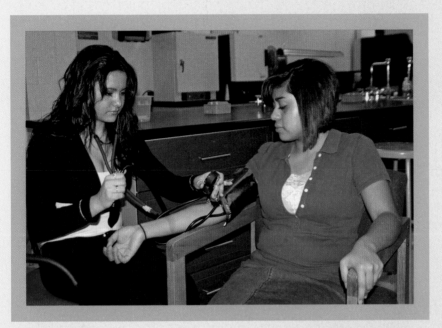

This young scientist is measuring blood pressure. A medical student taught her how to check human vital signs.

Simple observational experiments involving exotic animals may be possible. If you're interested in zoo animals, send a copy of your research plan to the zoo director and head veterinarian. Avoid elaborate requests that will affect how the zoo runs or take too much supervision from zoo staff.

How to Get Help from Mentors

Consider the magnetic ball and dog collar for retrievers that was discussed in the opening of this chapter. To make the most of their device, these students needed the support of an engineering mentor. How do students write a letter requesting help?

Read the sample letter in Figure 8.1, which could be sent to either an engineering department at a university or a professional engineer from the community.

Since scientific professionals use e-mail for most of their daily communications, send two copies of the letter, one via the postal service and the other through e-mail. The formal letter (postal service) shows that you are professional and serious about your project.

After a reasonable amount of time, consider following up with a phone call. *Note: E-mail messages from unfamiliar addresses are often not received by scientific professionals. Some messages are accidentally filtered out to help reduce "spam" (junk e-mail and advertisements). That's why a letter sent via regular mail is a good idea.*

This high school scientist wanted to study the behavior of exotic cats. She submitted her ideas to the local zoo. The zoo veterinarian and animal care staff helped her create a plan to collect observational data on behavior. This student's research helped the zoo find new ways to keep these captive animals stimulated.

FIGURE 8.1

Sample Letter Written to Ask for Mentorship

September 10, 2009
John Doe, Ph.D.
Professor, Department of Engineering
University of California Irvine
Irvine, CA 92111

Dear Dr. Doe:

I am a student at Arlington High School in Riverside, California. I am writing to request your help with a science fair project. My partner and I are trying to create an automatic ball thrower to entertain dogs. The device comes in two parts: 1) a magnetic dog collar and 2) a ball that contains a large magnet. We have a working prototype but need some help making improvements.

Currently, the ball has a magnet inside that is large and moves freely each time the ball is thrown. This is a problem because the weight of the magnet is not evenly distributed inside the ball. We know this affects how the ball travels when it is repelled by the magnetic collar. The uneven weight of the ball may also be unappealing to the dogs we test. We feel it is important to create a ball that's as similar as possible in weight and feel to a normal ball (such as a tennis ball).

We would be truly grateful for any help you can offer. If you have any information on mechanical devices or parts that could be used in this project, please let us know. My partner and I would be willing to meet at your office or we can correspond through e-mail.

For more information about this project, please refer to the attached engineering plan. Please let us know if you can help or know someone else who would be willing to mentor the final phases of this project.

If you have any further questions about us or this project, feel free to contact our science teacher, Mrs. Haven (e-mail: MHaven@email.com). We look forward to hearing from you and promise not to take too much of your time.

Thank you for your time and consideration of this request.

Sincerely,

Josh Martin   Lucrecia Jones
e-mail: jmartin@email.com   e-mail: ljones@email.com

Ten Steps to Create Your Own Mentor Request Letter

1. **Salutations: Dear *title* + *surname***
   Be sure to use the appropriate title.
   - Dear Dr. Carl:
     To address medical doctors (M.D.) or scientists with a doctorate (Ph.D.)
   - Dear Sir or Madam:
     When addressing "a general person," where you don't know an exact name
   - Dear Mr. Carl or Ms. Carl:
     When addressing a professional who does not have an M.D. or Ph.D. degree

2. **Introduce yourself.**
   I am a student at . . .

3. **Why are you writing (what kind of help do you need)?**
   I am writing to request your help with a science fair project.

4. **Provide a general introduction to the project.**

5. **Explain the problems you're trying to solve and need help with.**
   This will help the person understand what you need and how he or she may be able to help.

6. **How will you and the mentor communicate and exchange information?**
   Most professionals will prefer e-mail.

7. **Include a complete copy of your research or engineering plan.**

8. **If the person you're writing to isn't able to help, ask that person to forward the request to someone else.**

9. **Include a teacher contact from your school.**
   If you have any further questions about us or this project, feel free to contact our science teacher, Mrs. Haven (e-mail: _____).

10. **Closing. Thank the person and provide your contact information.**

Thank You Notes

Mentors want to know how the project came out and how you did at the science fair. Thanking your mentor is very important. You may need your adviser's help on another project in the future. Mentors can also provide a letter of recommendation for a future job or college application. Plus, everyone appreciates a "thank you."

Write a nice card in your best penmanship:

- Thank the mentor for his or her support.
- Tell your advisers how their guidance helped improve the project.
- List and describe any awards received in the science fair and let them know if the project will be advancing to higher levels of competition.
- Mention any plans to continue to develop and improve the project.
- Tell how this experience has added to your science education.
- Send a copy of the final research report and pictures of the poster with your thank you.

Surround yourself with great mentors. It always makes things easier to ask someone who has experience in the field you are working in. In my case, this was very important. Had I surrounded myself with good mentors earlier on, many of my rockets wouldn't have exploded, including one disaster right in our home kitchen.

—Siya Xuza

CHAPTER 9

The Research Report: Clear, Concise, and Credible

A research report is used to share the results from experiments or engineering projects. Professional scientists write reports that are published in scientific journals. These reports are often reviewed, anonymously, by peers from the research community. Scientists also showcase important information from a report on a scientific poster to reveal their findings to other scientists at national and international conferences. Similarly, student scientists also share their research in reports and posters when participating in science competitions.

In general, science fair judges are members of the scientific community. They look at your research report to learn how well you understand the scientific process and to find out more details about your project. This information should be laid out in the report in sections that are easy to find.

Most reports will include the following sections:
1. Title Page
2. Table of Contents
3. Abstract (some competitions)

4. Introduction
5. Materials and Methods
6. Results
7. Discussion and Conclusions
8. Future Investigation (optional)
9. References
10. Appendixes (optional)
11. Acknowledgments (not allowed in some competitions)

Parts of a Research Report

TITLE PAGE
- Title as it also appears on the poster
- Presented to the <year>, <name of science fair competition>
- <First and last name>, <Grade #>
- <Name and address of school>

TABLE OF CONTENTS

ABSTRACT (REQUIRED FOR CERTAIN SCIENCE FAIRS)

An abstract is a short summary (generally 250 words or less) of the important facts about the research or engineering project and the results. Write your abstract after your research report is complete. Use a highlighter to identify key sentences in your report. Copy and paste these sentences together to create a rough draft of the abstract. Clean up, shorten, and rearrange sentences and you'll be done.

WHAT SHOULD BE INCLUDED IN AN ABSTRACT?

- **Objectives:** State hypothesis and questions or engineering goal and purpose.
- **Materials and Methods:** Briefly discuss the main materials and procedures that were used. Include important details such as the number of research subjects.
- **Results and Conclusions:** Summarize the most important results and discuss how results relate to the original hypothesis. Engineers and computer scientists should discuss the device, how well it works, and whether the design goal was met.

INTRODUCTION

Good news! If you wrote a literature review for your research plan, you already have a rough draft of the introduction. Introduce the project and provide background information that will help readers understand your research. Provide clear and concise explanations that will help any reader understand the project regardless of their knowledge.

- **Background:** Include historic discoveries and research related to your project. Use and cite credible references. If the research has continued over several years, introduce prior work and discuss how your past studies have influenced the current project.

- **Purpose:** Tell why the study is important. What value does this research or engineering device have for our world? Include references that provide background about the topic—what is known and what is unknown.
- **Hypothesis:** State the hypothesis and questions that you were seeking to test.
- **Engineering Goal:** Explain what you were trying to create. Were you successful in engineering a working prototype?

MATERIALS AND METHODS

If you have a thorough experimental design or engineering plan, some of the work is already done. Change the writing to the past tense, update the information, and you have it! Provide enough details so that someone else could repeat the experiments and get the same results.

- **Materials:** Create a bulleted list or provide very specific descriptions of the materials that were used during experimentation or construction (engineering). Include the source or manufacturer of any unusual materials.
- **Methods:** *Be sure to write all of the procedures in the past tense.*

  Experimental research: Explain how experiments were designed and run.

  Engineering projects: Explain what the final design and construction of the prototype involved. Was the prototype tested? If so, include a section that covers testing procedures and explains how tests were documented (video camera, time trials, or something else) and if any data were collected. When possible, include diagrams, flow charts, and photos. However, there is no substitute for written explanations.

RESULTS

What belongs in the results section? The results section can include tables, graphs, photographs, and drawings that report results from experimental or engineering efforts. Label images (graphs, photos, diagrams) in order, beginning with Figure 1. Include a legend that briefly explains each figure. Tables should include a title and be labeled Table 1, Table 2, and so on. Number tables in their own sequence, separate from figures.

What doesn't belong in the results section? Avoid discussing the meaning of data in the results section. The purpose of this section is to display the most important data in ways that are easily understood, such as graphs, tables, or pictures. Text can describe any results that are not shown in a table or graph.

DISCUSSION

- **Experimental research:** Discuss the meaning of data from the results section. What do data reveal about the original hypothesis and questions? Was the hypothesis supported or refuted? Always cite specific figures and tables in the body of your discussion. Were there any problems that could have affected the results? How could those problems be addressed in future experiments? When appropriate, suggest alternative hypotheses that could be tested in future experiments.

- **Engineering projects:** Discuss difficulties, changes, and improvements to the original design. Does the prototype work and, if so, how well does it work? Did you achieve the original design goal?

Link information from the results section to the discussion section. For example, refer to Figure 1 in the text of the discussion when you are explaining that part of the experimental results.

CONCLUSIONS (OPTIONAL)

A brief, separate conclusions section can be used to summarize the main findings. To make the conclusions stand out, highlight the conclusions in a short, bulleted list.

FUTURE INVESTIGATION (OPTIONAL)

A separate section may be added to explore new experimental ideas or engineering design improvements that expand on the original project. This section should be brief. Otherwise, summarize ideas for future investigation in the discussion.

REFERENCES

Check the guidelines for listing and formatting references for the specific science competitions you enter. If you have a choice, select a style and stick with it. Some common formats are the APA (American

Psychological Association) and the MLA (Modern Language Association).

Some Web sites (see p. 157) allow you to select a format (APA, MLA, and others), then asks for specifics about your reference. The site will then format each reference for you, but beware: It won't correct your errors. If you misspell a name or enter the wrong date, the mistake stays with you.

Here are some samples of credible references:

- ELEMENTARY/MIDDLE SCHOOL: Encyclopedias (current and updated), textbooks, interviews, scientific organizations (Web sites), newspapers, weekly news magazines (e.g., *Time*), science magazines, and others.

- HIGH SCHOOL: *Scientific American* magazine, *Discover* magazine, the weekly *New York Times* "Science Times" section, Environmental Protection Agency (Web site). Students who advance to national or international competitions should also include references from scientific journals (available through college libraries and the magazine database search engines of public libraries).

Student scientists should avoid using online encyclopedias that allow users to write and edit reference information. Because articles and definitions aren't necessarily written by experts, these sources are not reliable. If you find something interesting on one of these sites, be sure to verify information from a reliable source that is written and edited by experts. Refer to Appendix 1 for tips on using the Internet to find reliable references.

APPENDIXES (OPTIONAL)

Use this section to provide definitions, large data tables, questionnaires, and detailed schematics. Don't put everything that's not in the report in an appendix. Provide only information that's important and will help make your report clearer and more credible.

ACKNOWLEDGMENTS

Write a short paragraph to thank mentors, businesses, or college departments that helped with the project. Include the mentors' correct titles and business affiliations.

Scientific Writing Is Clear, Concise, and Credible

- **Clear:** *Accurately stated or described.* Avoid unnecessary details and extra adjectives. Use diagrams, tables, and graphs to explain construction or experimentation.
- **Concise:** *Explaining things in a few words; clear and succinct.* Focus on the facts. The writing should resemble explanations from an encyclopedia or science textbook. Long, wordy explanations detract from the scientific information and data readers need to understand.

- **Credible:** *Worthy of belief; trustworthy.* Back your research and conclusions with enough data. In the introduction, reference methods used in similar studies, historic research, and other important discoveries.

Back to the Basics: Important Writing Tips

- Write the report on a computer and always use the spell checker.
- Format the report in the standard way:
    Font: Black type, Times New Roman/12-point
    Margins: 1½ inches from the top of the page; 1 inch from the sides and bottom of page

ELEMENTARY AND MIDDLE SCHOOL STUDENTS: Unless your teacher says otherwise, it's okay to use *I* or *we* when writing the report but try not to overdo it.

HIGH SCHOOL STUDENTS: Write in the passive voice. Avoid overuse of the words *I* and *we*. Limited use of *I* and *we* is okay in the introduction and discussion.

First person, active voice: I studied how three lawn fertilizers affected common soil-dwelling insects.

Third person, passive voice: The effect of three lawn fertilizers on common soil-dwelling insects was studied.

Good practices for science writing:

- Avoid using contractions.
    The sow bug population *wasn't* affected.
    The sow bug population *was not* affected.

- Write in the past tense. You are reporting on experiments and work that were done in the past.
  Present tense: The plants *are* grown under ultra-violet lights.
  Past tense: Plants *were* grown under ultraviolet lights.
- Keep most of the sentences short and to the point.

Descriptive Storytelling Versus Revealing Facts From a Scientific Study

Elaborate descriptions have a place in the scientific journal (project notebook), but not in the final research report. Keep your readers focused on the science by writing *clear* and *concise* sentences. Two fictitious writing samples follow; both attempt to provide readers with the location of a water sampling site. Read the passages below. Then decide which one presents information that is *clear*, *concise*, and *credible*.

Example 1: For my project, I collected and tested water samples from six different sites along the banks of the Spanish Fork River. All of the sites were located more or less 3 miles south of Route 11. A trailhead to my sites is marked by a decaying "Bob's Big Boy Restaurant" billboard. Once the river is in sight, you can see a maze of puddles that meander between lush native grasses creating a rich, wetland environment.

Example 2: Water samples were collected from six sites along the Spanish Fork River. The sites were located approximately 3 miles south of Route 11. Native grasses and wetlands extended approximately 15 feet from the banks of the river.

The first passage is wordy and relies on visual landmarks to relocate the sampling site. Given this information alone, would you be able to find the sampling site?

For every science fair you enter remember to
- check report-formatting guidelines.
  Most science competitions have detailed submission guidelines available online.
- edit and improve the report for each new competition. *Note: Be sure any changes to the report are included in the text of the poster.*
- watch for page limits.

●●●●●●●●●●●●●●●●●●

Science Competitions

If we all did the things we are capable of, we would astound ourselves.

—Thomas Edison

For some students, research and science fairs are like an academic sport. Both physical and mental athletes work hard and improve their skills with practice. Give research a try. Most students are surprised by how much fun it is to be a scientist and make new discoveries. If this academic sport is for you, stick with it. The top student scientists work on projects for several years (read more about three top student scientists in Chapter 2) and enter multiple science competitions along the way.

Science Competitions: An Important Part of the Research Experience

From experimental research to engineering, science fair participants get an unprecedented look at the scientific process and career opportunities in the sciences. In fact, student research experience mirrors what professional scientists do every day.

When professional scientists make new discoveries, they often share their findings at scientific meetings. These meetings are a lot like student science competitions. The research project is either displayed on a poster or presented orally, usually in a slide presentation.

Once your science fair project is finished, sharing your work with others is a reward. Get the most out of your research experience by entering your project into as many science competitions as possible. Of course, remember to always put your schoolwork first.

Two Types of Research Competitions

SCIENCE FAIRS

Some science competitions ask students to communicate research findings using a scientific poster (at a science fair). Others require students to submit their report through the mail. Judges evaluate projects based on scientific merit, student knowledge, and presentation skills (oral or written).

RESEARCH REPORT COMPETITIONS

Top projects are usually selected to compete for prizes and scholarships at regional, national, or international student research conferences. These competitions allow students to meet with other young scientists and experts. The events also include behind-the-scenes scientific tours and other fun science activities. And the best part: If you're picked as a finalist, the trip and activities are usually free.

Science Fair Competition

Every community's science fair opportunities are different. Most students get started at a school or district science fair. The top projects are then selected to move up to the next level of competition. Some states have a state science competition while others have two or more regional science competitions.

Your state's science fair competition ladder may involve some or all of the following steps:

- school science fair
- district science fair
- regional science fair
- state science fair
- national and international science competitions

If your school doesn't have a science fair, you'll need to enter a district or regional competition.

To learn how science fair competitions are organized in your state, ask a science teacher or contact the science specialist for your school district or state public education system.

Major Research Competitions

Are you an academic athlete? Get the most out of your project and research experience by learning about the

This sixth grade student's display included news articles and photos. The information helped judges to understand the scope and importance of her topic.

different science competitions. Understanding how to enter a science competition and finding out about all the different research competitions can be difficult. The list that follows provides examples of some of the better-known science contests and includes Web addresses.

Find the science competitions that you qualify to enter or wish to target and then ask parents and teachers to help you understand the rules and complete the entry forms. Filling in the application correctly is very important. Mistakes or missing forms can lead to disqualification (and missed opportunities).

ELEMENTARY AND MIDDLE SCHOOL

Similar to high school students, elementary and middle school students usually begin by presenting a project at a school science fair. The best projects are then selected to compete at local and state competitions. Beyond this, the top projects in the state are invited to enter the best-known national competition for elementary and middle school students, sponsored by the Society for Science & the Public (formerly known as the Discovery Channel Young Scientist Challenge).

The Society for Science & the Public (SSP) Middle School Program (http://sciserv.org/msp/Index.asp) is to student scientists in grades 5–8 as the Intel International Science and Engineering Fair is to high school scientists. The application process includes a series of essays about the student and his or her research project. The young scientist's inspiration, interests,

At the regional or state science fair, student scientists compete for awards, scholarships, and a chance to advance to national and international science fairs.

and life experiences are considered. Prizes include gift certificates and scholarships. Finalists travel, all expenses paid, to Washington, D.C., and compete for over $40,000 in scholarships and awards.

HIGH SCHOOL

International Science and Engineering Fair (ISEF)
<http://www.societyforscience.org/isef/index.asp>
AND **<http://www.intel.com/education/isef/index**
.htm>

The International Science and Engineering Fair (ISEF) is the Olympics of science fairs. Nearly 1,500 students from nearly 50 countries compete for prizes, trips, and scholarships. Awards for team and individual entries

Science fairs are a time to celebrate. At the opening ceremony of the 2007 International Science and Engineering Fair, students participate in a "Shout-Out." Students representing almost fifty countries created banners and waved flags before a crowd of 6,000 people, showing support for each other and their scientific efforts.

range from $500 to $50,000, and total nearly $4 million. In the United States, the top student scientists are selected from regional and state science fairs to travel to ISEF, all expenses paid.

- Learn more about the range and depth of projects that compete at ISEF by purchasing an Abstract Book. Each year abstracts from the 1,500 finalists are published. Ordering information is available, online, in the ISEF document library (<http://sciserv.org/isef/document>).

- Find the science fairs in your state that select projects to advance to ISEF at <http://www.sciserv.org/isef/students/aff_fairsearch.asp>.

Siya Xuza represents South Africa at the 2007 International Science and Engineering Fair.

Intel Science Talent Search (STS)
<http://www.societyforscience.org/sts/index.asp>

Intel Science Talent Search is the oldest and most prestigious research contest in the United States. In fact, it's sometimes referred to as the "Junior Nobel Prize." Each year, 40 finalists (individual projects only) are selected from thousands of entries to present at the weeklong Science Talent Institute in Washington, D.C. Over $1,000,000 in prizes are awarded, and the top prize is a $100,000 scholarship.

Siemens Competition in Math, Science, and Technology
<http://www.siemens-foundation.org/en/ competition.htm>

Approximately 1,100 individual and team projects are submitted to Siemens each year. Student scientists travel to a regional host university, all expenses paid, to present their research and to compete for scholarships and a chance to continue on to the national Siemens competition. Siemens doesn't accept behavioral or social science projects. Over $2,000,000 in scholarships are awarded.

Junior Science and Humanities Symposium (JSHS)
<http://www.jshs.org>

Each year, over 30 regional symposia are hosted by universities around the country. The symposia are multiday events. Qualifying entries are selected to present research, either as a poster or orally (in a slide presentation). Top projects are awarded scholarships through JSHS and the hosting university. Symposium winners are then invited, all expenses paid, to present at the National JSHS, sponsored by the U.S. Army, Navy, and Air Force. Scholarships range from $500 to $16,000 for multiple winners at each level of JSHS competition. The national JSHS winners are invited to present their work at the London International Science Youth Forum (<http://www.liysf.org.uk/index.asp>) where they have an opportunity to meet outstanding student scientists from 60 countries.

Other High School Research Competitions

- The Stockholm Junior Water Prize (SJWP) http://www.wef.org/AboutWater/ForStudents/SJWP>
- International Sustainable World (Energy, Engineering, and Environment) (I-SWEEP) <http://www.isweep.org>
- American Museum of Natural History: Young Naturalist Awards <http://www.amnh.org/nationalcenter/youngnaturalistawards>
- Young Epidemiology Scholars Competition (YES) <http://www.collegeboard.com/yes/fs/atc.html>

Research Competitions (All Ages)

Davidson Fellows Scholarships
<http://www.davidsongifted.org/fellows>

There are no minimum age requirements for this competition. Winning projects are awarded scholarships from $25,000 to $50,000. Human and animal studies are not allowed.

Team America Rocketry Challenge
<http://www.aia-aerospace.org/tarc/index.cfm>
Students in grades 7 to 12 are invited to participate in the largest rocket competition in the world. The top ten teams share $60,000 in cash and scholarships.

It's impossible to list all of the research and scholarship competitions available to young scientists today. Automobile manufacturers and national engineering and medical associations, as well as private companies, often offer their own scholarship and research competitions.

Selling the Science: Poster and Presentation

Most students have fun moving from research to "selling their science" in a poster display or slide presentation. Enter a science fair and showcase your hard work and discoveries. Taking the time to create a clear and visually pleasing presentation is important. Your presentation is the first step in capturing the attention and interest of teachers and science fair judges. Make them want to know more about your research project!

Designing a Poster Display

The main ingredient for making a great poster is a well-written research report (see Chapter 9). The poster should provide a visually pleasing and concise presentation of the research process followed in your project. Begin by making sure your research report is free of grammatical errors. Most, if not all, of the sections in your research paper can be modified and used on the poster. The main sections of a scientific poster are broken down for experimental and engineering projects in Figure 11.1.

The clever display for "Better Bumpers" let judges and visitors know that this physics project had something to do with improving the bumpers on cars. Get creative with the lettering, colors, and organization of your display.

Reformatting the Research Report for the Poster Display

With the research completed and the report written, it's easy to cut information and change the font size to create a poster display. The poster is an overview of the project. It should be long enough to supply visitors with general information about each part of the project, but not so long that visitors will not read it. Include on your poster the main points from the introduction and discussion sections of your research report. Avoid

123

FIGURE 11.1

Headings and Sections for the Poster Display

Experimental Projects: Title

Question/Hypothesis

Use bullets if you have several hypotheses.

Introduction

Include essential background on prior research and basic facts relevant to your project.
* Is the project a continuation of work from other years? If so, include a brief summary of the prior research and explain how it affected the current project.

Materials & Methods

Create a bulleted list of the materials. Outline key procedures. In some cases, diagrams or photos are a nice addition.

Acknowledgements

Note: Some science fairs do not allow acknowledgments on the poster.

Results (Figures)

Create a visually pleasing, easy-to-read display of tables, graphs, and photographs. These figures tell people what was learned from the experiments.
*Avoid repetitive presentations of data. Don't display a table when the data are shown in a graph, and don't display multiple graphs of the same data.

Discussion

Restate the hypothesis.
Discuss whether results support or refute the hypothesis. Discuss unexpected results, experimental failures, or mistakes that were made.

References

List references according to science fair guidelines.

Future Investigation

Briefly discuss improvements, alternative hypotheses, and ideas for expanding the project.

FIGURE 11.1 *continued*

Engineering Project-Title

Problem/Design Goal

State the problem or design goal. State the intended purpose or function of the device.

Introduction

State why this device is important.

Discuss related devices, how they were constructed, and how they work.

Is the project a continuation of work from other years? If so, include a brief summary of the prior research and explain how it affected the current project.

Materials and Design

Create a bulleted list of the materials. Include a labeled schematic or flow chart to show how the device was constructed. In some cases, photos are a nice addition.

Provide a history that shows the phases of construction that led to the final prototype.

Acknowledgements

*Some science fairs do not allow acknowledgments on the poster.

Results

Tell how well the prototype functions.

Explain whether the device functions according to the design goal. Provide data to support how well it works.

Present test data in graphs and tables.

Consider including photographs that show important changes and improvements made during construction.

Discussion

Restate the design goal.

Discuss changes that were needed to meet or get close to achieving the original design goal.

Discuss problems with the prototype.

References

List references according to science fair guidelines.

Future

Briefly outline changes that could improve the design and function of the prototype. Discuss ideas for future generations of prototypes.

repetition. Delete or shorten sentences wherever possible. Your poster should provide a less detailed version of the methods and procedures than your research report.

The process begins by editing and reformatting the text from your report on the computer. Before editing begin by creating a new computer file. Copy the report and rename it "poster text."

1. Reformat each section of the report for display on the poster.
   - Choose a font that is easy to read (such as Arial or Times New Roman).
   - Enlarge the text so that it can be read from a distance of 3 feet.
   - Where appropriate, use bulleted lists to present *multiple hypotheses* or *engineering goals, materials, and methods*

2. Emphasize data and results.
   - Include well-labeled, visually pleasing graphs to showcase data.
   - Display only those data that are important to understanding the hypotheses or goals of the project. All other data should be in the research report and project notebook.

3. In addition to the poster display, always include (on the display table)
   - a complete copy of the research report
   - the original project notebook (or a photocopy if there is any chance the notebook could be lost)

The author visits one of her students, who participated in the 2006 International Science and Engineering Fair. Each section of the research report was reformatted for the poster display.

Using Photographs on a Scientific Poster

Photographs and diagrams help tell the research story. They are eye-catching elements that make visitors want to learn more about a project. Include a caption with each photo to answer these questions:

- What is the picture about?
- Who took the picture (Photo taken by…)?
- When and where was the photograph taken?

To display pictures of a person or people, you need their permission. Minors need parental consent. Regional, national, and international science fairs have very specific rules about displaying photos that show people. Always be sure to check contest rules.

The Right Poster Board

Premade poster boards are available in a variety of colors. **Where can you buy poster board?**

- Retail stores. Try craft stores (such as Michaels or Roberts Crafts), discount houses (such as Wal-Mart), and drug stores (such as Walgreens). Such stores typically carry only one board size in limited colors. Students can also build their own display using lightweight materials such as foam core.
- Showboard.com (<http://www.showboard.com>), which specializes in poster boards and science fair materials. Their boards come in a large array of

sizes and colors, and the company will ship orders directly to your home or school. Keep the shipping box. It's a great way to transport the finished scientific poster to any science fair you enter.

What size board do you need? Choosing the right size and color is important. A board that is too big will make it look as if you didn't do much work on the project, and a board that is too small can be so crammed with information that it's difficult to read. Science fairs and teachers may limit the board size and materials allowed on the poster display. Before buying a board, check with your teacher or read the rules for science fairs you plan to enter.

- Elementary and middle school students can usually choose a board that is 36″ × 36″ or 48″ × 48″. Use any color; be creative and have fun.
- High school scientists have opportunities to advance to regional, national, and international competition. For each level of competition, the rules vary. In general, the most dedicated scientists redesign their boards for each science fair.

Check with your school, district, and regional science fair organizers to decide on the right size for your project display. If you have enough information and data, always use the biggest board allowed. The maximum size allowed at the Intel International Science and Engineering Fair is 30″ deep × 48″ wide × 108″ high (measured from the floor to the top of the poster).

Pick a color that won't be a distraction. Some of the best color choices are black, light blue, navy blue, or dark green.

Designing the Board: Scrapbooking Secrets

Scrapbooking can be used to create interesting, attention-grabbing displays. Most scrapbooking stores have a complimentary workroom where you'll find tools like die cuts (to cut shapes) and slide cutters for trimming papers. Slide cutters are also readily available at local printing shops (such as FedEx-Kinko's).

Where to go for help, ideas, and supplies:

- local scrapbooking shop
- craft store
- online stores for scrapbookers and crafters
- showboard.com (www.showboard.com)

SOME DISPLAY IDEAS

- Create the title and headings using sturdy cardstock.
- Use a stencil to outline letters and then cut them out.
- Use a die cut or other machine to create custom letters.
- Purchase packages of precut letters.
- Mount letters of a title or heading on individual circles or squares to make them stand out or just glue them onto a colorful strip of cardstock.
- Display diagrams or maps.
- Use high-quality markers or a computer to create a basic map or diagram.

Are Little League baseball players getting stressed out by their parents? When a project is about something popular and well known, consider incorporating the theme into the poster. This poster included cutouts of baseballs and bats.

- Use string and colorful pins to connect locations on a map or diagram.
- Create a three-dimensional effect by using Zots or similar adhesive mounting pads to make letters, photos, or other display items pop up.
- Save space by displaying important information in a flip chart. Place the most important information on the top of the chart to be sure that it will be the first thing the science fair judges see.
- Create a booklet of related information and use brads to attach the booklet to the board. This is good for:
  - large sets of data (graphs, tables, etc.)

- series of photographs
- engineering projects: steps followed to assemble the device

Never attach food, liquids, plant material, or any other dead or living thing to the poster. Most science fairs don't allow students to display such things. Ask your teacher if your school fair makes any exceptions.

SUPPLIES

Before getting started, collect these "must-have" poster supplies:

- poster board (purchase, order, or build)
- white paper and two or three colors of 12" × 12" scrapbook cardstock or standard construction paper (Never use more than three colors. Too many can be distracting.)
- adhesive mounting pads or Zots
- slide cutter and scissors
- T-square or right-angle ruler and yardstick (meterstick)
- colored markers
- glue stick (not repositionable, which tends to fail) (Never use liquid glues for mounting. Paper tends to ripple and bump.)
- double-stick tape
- letter stencils or precut letters

Creating a Poster Display

Your layout can vary, but information should always flow and follow the research process from beginning to

132

end. Before attaching anything to the final poster board, use a large piece of paper to plan the layout. And then when you're ready to start attaching things to the board always use a T-square or other devices to make sure the information is mounted straight. Use the layout of information in Figure 11.1 to begin designing your poster.

DISPLAY ITEMS

At the display table always include
- a complete copy of the research report (along with any human subject questionnaires)
- the original project notebook (and original research data, computer programming code, etc.)
- a copy of the abstract (Note: Abstracts aren't required at every science fair.)

DISPLAYING INFORMATION FROM MORE THAN ONE YEAR OF RESEARCH

If your project is selected to advance to a regional, national, or international science fair competition, learn the rules! In the Intel International Science and Engineering Fair, multiyear projects may display project notebooks for research done over several years. Prior, relevant work may also be included in the introduction. However, only data completed during the current academic year may be included on the poster board.

DEMONSTRATION AND OTHER DISPLAY ITEMS

Whenever possible and appropriate to the project, young scientists should include demonstration or display items with their poster. These items add interest and give visitors an up-close look at the project.

WHAT CAN YOU DO TO IMPROVE YOU PROJECT DISPLAY?

Ideas for an experimental research project: If the experiment can be demonstrated, include hands-on demonstration items. If not, consider creating a short film documenting what happened in the experiments. Display film on a laptop and run it continuously, on a loop.

Example: Film animal subjects such as mice, dogs, or birds during an experiment.

If the project involved human subjects, invite visitors to try the experiment. Include puzzles, surveys, or other testing materials and then keep track of the results. Show visitors results by inputting data into a computer spreadsheet and graphing.

Ideas for an engineering project: If the device is small enough to display or can be demonstrated, include it. Otherwise, be sure to create a short demonstration film that can be run, continuously, from a laptop computer.

Ideas for computer projects: Computer projects should always be demonstrated. Bring a backup copy of any files, and if possible, a backup computer. Computer projects involve either programming or construction.

- Programming: Demonstrate the working program and have copies and files of the programming language available for judges and visitors to review.
- Construction: Display the working system or bring video footage to demonstrate how things work.

Sample Project Displays

Deadly Waters; Shannon Lisa Babb (Twelfth grade); 2006, Intel International Science and Engineering Fair
Data are presented in flip charts to save space.

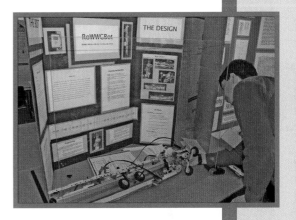

Robotic Window Washer for Glass Buildings; Daniel Blakemore (Tenth grade); 2007, Salt Lake Science and Engineering Fair
A piece of Plexiglas creates a demonstration window in front of the project. The robotic window washer is suspended from the glass and ready for demonstration.

African Space; Siya Yuza 2007, Intel International Science and Engineering Fair
Demonstration items include a rocket hull and launch stands.

●●●●●●●●●●●●●●●●●●●●●●

Get Ready for Judging at the Science Fair

Once the experiments are finished, the report is written, and the poster has been created, you're ready to meet the judges. One high school scientist had a great experience at the science fair and truly enjoyed talking with judges, something she didn't expect. Her story follows.

The student spit out her gum, turned off her iPod, and tucked in her shirt before proudly taking her place next to her research poster. Her mind was filled with excitement and anticipation, but her stomach was full of butterflies. Five judges would visit her project that day. The poster invited judges with an artistic layout and intriguing title, "Colorful Comprehension." She had prepared what she wanted to say. She had read and reread her research report many times, and she carried with her a small stack of note cards. While she waited, she wondered, "Will the judges like my project? What if I can't answer a question? What will they think?"

One by one the judges visited her project. After the first judge's visit, she placed her wrinkled and sweaty pile of note cards under the display table, out of sight. She didn't need the cards. The judges just wanted to

This student dressed professionally and was well prepared. She used the graphs and information on her poster to explain her project to judges.

talk to her. She used the display board to state her question, "Does text color influence reading comprehension?" She talked about how the experiments were designed, and she used graphs to discuss the results. She never used the speech she had practiced. Each judge was genuinely interested in the work she had done. The judges offered suggestions to improve the study and encouraged her interest in research and the sciences. When the last judge had finished, she was sad that the fair was over.

How Will Your Project Be Judged?

Judges are volunteers who are excited to meet with student scientists. They are interested in what you've accomplished, and they want to encourage your continued scientific curiosity. However, the judging process can differ depending on who the judges are and how the science fair is organized.

JUDGING AT A SCHOOL SCIENCE FAIR

- ### ELEMENTARY AND MIDDLE SCHOOL SCIENCE FAIRS
  Judges are typically teachers, parents (with science degrees), or college students (majoring in science and working on a bachelor's, master's, or Ph.D.). Parents who serve as judges are not allowed to judge their own children.

- ### HIGH SCHOOL SCIENCE FAIRS
  Judges are typically engineers, physicians, medical students, scientists, or doctoral students from the community or a local university. The higher the level of science fair competition, the more qualified the judges. At national and international science fairs, expect experts to judge your project. For example, projects competing in the physics category are assigned to physicists who specialize in

mechanics, electricity, particle physics, or astrophysics, depending on the student's research focus.

THE JUDGING PROCESS

Judging standards and scoring methods are created for every science fair. The scoring categories and grading system are organized into a rubric. Rubrics exist to help judges keep the scoring process as fair as possible. Table 12.1 is an example of a scoring system that judges may use at a science fair. Consider using it in your own self-evaluation before the science fair.

Before judges meet with students, judges read and evaluate projects during a judge preview session.

TABLE 12.1

Example of a Science Fair Score Sheet*

PROJECT	DESCRIPTION	POINTS POSSIBLE	SELF EVALUATION	JUDGE EVALUATIC
ABSTRACT	50–250 words, fully summarizes experiment.	5		
INTRODUCTION	Clearly identifies the problem, including statement/question/purpose. Provides background information. Project is appropriate for grade level.	10		
HYPOTHESIS	Is testable and written as a statement.	5		
MATERIALS	Complete list.	5		
EXPERIMENTAL PROCEDURE	Concise, step-by-step directions. If a control is needed, it's clearly identified. Variables that aren't part of the experiment but could affect results are controlled.	15		
RESULTS/ ANALYSIS OF DATA	Includes sufficient number of trials. Data are directly related to hypothesis. Photographs of the experiment in progress (optional but enhance project). Graphs and charts are directly related to experiment. Graphs and charts are correctly shown, appropriate for data, and make sense.	15		
CONCLUSION	Purpose/hypothesis restated. States if hypothesis is supported or not. Data used to explain whether hypothesis is supported. Discusses other factors or errors that might have affected the results. Includes unexpected findings. Discusses possible real-world applications for project. States what new questions came up. States ideas for advancing the project.	10		
REFERENCES	At least five bibliographic references, properly formatted.	5		
DISPLAY	Display board is neat, organized, and easy to follow; few or no spelling, grammar, or punctuation errors.	10		

CREATIVITY	Research area or topic is novel to student and audience. Approach to the testing shows creativity. Intrepretation of data is reasonable and thorough. Display arrangement is eye-catching and interesting.	10		
ORAL PRESENTATION	Student was prepared and well practiced. Student clearly describes what was done and demonstrates knowledge and under-standing of the topic, experimental design, and data.	10		

*Adapted and reprinted courtesy of Salt Lake City School District.

ISEF Judging

The Intel International Science and Engineering Fair (ISEF) is the world's largest pre-college science competition. (Refer to Chapter 10 for more information about ISEF.) Thus, this fair has some of the highest standards for selecting and preparing judges of any advanced research competition. Furthermore, state and regional science fairs that select students for ISEF follow the same guidelines. General information about what students can expect from judges at ISEF is given in Table 12.2.

Engineering Projects and Patents

Engineers beware! If you plan to take your device to the market place, consider filing for patent protection

TABLE 12.2

Judging Guidelines for the ISEF

Judges evaluate and focus on
- what the student did in the current year;
- how well scientific, engineering, computer programming, or mathematical methodologies were followed;
- the detail and accuracy of research as documented in the data book (notebook);
- whether experimental procedures were used in the best possible way.

Judges look for well-thought-out research. They look at how significant your project is in its field, how thorough you were, and how much of the experiment and design is your own work.

Initially, to learn about a project, judges get information from the poster, abstract, and research paper, but the *interview* is the final measure of your work.

Judges applaud those students who can speak freely and confidently about their work. They are not interested in memorized speeches or presentations; they simply want to talk with you about your research to see if you have a good grasp of your project from start to finish. It is important to start the interview off right.

Greet judges and introduce yourself. Appearance, good manners, appropriate attire, and enthusiasm for what you are doing will make a positive first impression.

Judges often ask questions, such as: "How did you come up with this idea?" "What didn't you do?" "What further plans do you have to continue this research?" and "What are the practical applications of your project?"

Remember, judges need to see if you understand the basic principles of science behind your project or topic area. They want to determine if you have correctly measured and analyzed data. They want to know if you can determine possible sources of error in your project. Finally, judges seek to encourage you in your scientific efforts and your future goals or career in science. Relax and enjoy your time to learn from them and accept their accolades for your fine work.

Intel ISEF Judging Criteria (points)

Creative ability	30	25
Scientific thought and engineering goals	30	25
Thoroughness	15	12
Skill	15	12
Clarity	10	10
Teamwork	—	16

*Permission to adapt and reprint ISEF judging guidelines is courtesy of Science Service. For more information about ISEF and Science Service, visit their Web site at http://sciserv.org/isef/about/background.asp

Mike Adamson talks with a judge about "An Extraordinary Light,"a lamp that also recharges batteries. Avoid memorizing your presentation. Judges just want to talk, ask you some questions, and encourage your interest in science.

before presenting at a science fair. One of the easiest things that you can do to protect your idea is to file an Invention Disclosure Form. You'll need help from an attorney, but this first step is inexpensive and will preserve your right to pursue a patent later on.

Law firms in your community may be willing to help by offering their services free of charge. You can find a wealth of information on patenting devices in the United States by visiting the U.S. Patent and Trademark Office Web site at (http://uspto.gov.).

Things to Remember When You're at a Science Fair

Science fairs celebrate student achievements in research and engineering. Be proud of your project and have fun

This student shares her findings with a science fair judge. She demonstrated how to measure vital lung capacity using a dry spirometer and then used the graphs and data on the poster to reveal her conclusions. "Breathe-in, Breathe-out" received a special award from Salt Lake City's Leonardo Science Center. With the student's help, the project will be developed into an interactive exhibit for the new Science Center.

at the science fair. Preparing for judging is the easy part of the process.

There are three main things to keep in mind when you are presenting:

1. Be confident.
2. Be proud, but humble.
3. Be knowledgeable.

The following tips will add the polish needed to help you get the most out of meeting with judges.

- Avoid memorizing and rehearsing a speech to give to judges. Just relax and share what you've accomplished in a friendly conversation.

- Do your best to answer questions and never fake an answer. It's okay to say, "I don't know." Judges recognize you can't know everything. They don't know everything either.

- Show interest in science by asking judges questions about your project and other scientific interests.

- Write the tips that the judges give you in your notebook. They may have ideas for improving the project or suggestions for fixing a problem with an experiment.

- The most important thing to remember is to have fun at the science fair!

Science is more than just equations. It's a lifestyle. Enjoy your research, challenge yourself, understand your results, communicate your ideas with others.

—Siya Xuza

APPENDIX 1:

References and Searching for Information

The right resources are important in finding an idea and learning background information. Reliable choices include textbooks, science magazines, and other references available through the public library. For the twenty-first century student scientist, the ultimate source for quick information is definitely the Internet. Learn how to get the most out of your Internet searches and take a look at the reference list at the end of this appendix for links to reputable sources of scientific information. *Note: Although the Internet is an amazing information resource, student scientists should never create a report that includes Internet references alone.*

Getting the Most Out of Your Internet Searches

There are two problems with the Internet:
1. finding reliable sources and knowing they are reliable
2. finding the right references when each search brings up hundreds of choices

"Google" It

Popular and well known, the search engine Google is easy to use. Other popular search engines include Yahoo, MSN, AOL, Ask, and AltaVista. You can find lots of information using any search engine, including information that is unreliable. The key to finding what you're looking for is to use the right terms and evaluate the sources.

Getting Started on a Fruitful Internet Search

Before starting to search on the Internet, learn scientific terminology related to your project. This is important because conversational words may not provide reliable information. High school and undergraduate college text-books are a great way to become familiar with terminology.

Consider the following topics and learn about some commonly used scientific terms.

- learning: *cognitive, recall, neuroscience, psychology*
- exercise, fitness, coordination, physical therapy: *developmental, physical tests, fine motor skills, gross motor skills, agility, neurological development, neurological connections, therapy, reflexes, reaction time, sports, athleticism*
- animals: *canine, feline, equine, reptiles, amphibians, species, warm-blooded animals, cold-blooded animals, mammals, nocturnal animals, aquatic, terrestrial*
- body temperature: *thermoregulation, temperature sensitivity, cooling, adaptation, heat exhaustion, evaporative cooling, poikilotherm, endotherm, ectotherm, gradient.*
- the heart: *cardiac, heart rate, pulse, vital signs, respiration, recovery rate, maximum heart rate, maximum cardiac output, physiological response, fitness, cardiac muscle, angiogram, electrocardiogram (EKG), three-chambered heart (birds and reptiles), four-chambered heart (mammals).*

- music: *tempo, rhythm, music types (classical, rap, pop, jazz, hip-hop, and others), hearing, acoustics, melody, harmony, sound waves, frequency, pitch*
- engines and mechanical devices (nonspecific): *exhaust, combustion, efficiency, emissions, load, stress, force, construction, design, analysis, dynamometer, accelerant, fuel, heat loss, catalysts, pressure, terms for parts of the engine, solar, hydrogen*

To Identify Reliable Online Sources

- **Look at *where* the information came from.** Reputable scientific sources, such as government, public or private educational groups, research institutions (often .gov or .edu sites)
- **Look at *who* authored the source.** Credentials: PhD, MD, psychiatrist, physical therapist, engineer

Whether you're looking for a project idea or references, the following information provides great sources for facts and scientific inspiration. *Note: If you find that one of these links is no longer active, try looking for the organization using your favorite search engine. Sometimes it's just a change of address (URL).*

GOVERNMENT AGENCIES

Many government agencies offer accurate, up-to-date scientific information that is easily understood. In some cases this includes access to large databases on everything from plants to the flu to cancer to global fish populations.

Entire science fair projects can be based on information from a database used to answer novel questions.

- Environmental Protection Agency (EPA)
  General information: <http://www.epa.gov>
  Educational resources:
  <http:// www.epa.gov/epahome/students.htm>
- National Science Foundation
  General information: <http://www.nsf.gov>
  Educational resources:
  <http://www.nsf.gov/news/classroom>
- National Oceanic and Atmospheric Administration
  General information: <http://www.noaa.gov>
  Educational resources: <http://www.education
  .noaa.gov>
- United States Geological Survey
  General information: <http://www.usgs.gov>
  Educator information: <http://education.usgs.gov>
- United States Department of Agriculture
  General information:
  <http://www.usda.gov/wps/portal/usdahome>

TELEVISION

- National News (NBC, ABC, CBS, CNN)
- Public Broadcasting System (PBS). Example: NOVA offers outstanding science shows. Programs are archived and some are available for online viewing. <http://www.pbs.org/wgbh/nova/programs>
- Scientific American Frontiers (view shows online): <http://www.pbs.org/saf>
- Discovery Channel
  MythBusters is a fun show that tests myths and urban legends using the scientific method.
  <http://dsc.discovery.com/fansites/mythbusters/mythbusters.html>

RADIO

- National Public Radio: *Science Friday*
  Science Friday is a weekly radio show that provides exciting, up-to-date coverage of current science news. The information is clearly presented. Visit their Web site for podcasts from past shows.
  <http://www.sciencefriday.com>

INTERNET

- How Stuff Works: <http://www.howstuffworks.com> and Instructables: <http://www.instructables.com>.
  Great sites for aspiring engineers. By learning how things work you can find new ideas and ways to repurpose existing technology in an engineering project.
- Science News Daily: <http://www.sciencenewsdaily.org>
- Science News for Kids:
  <http://www.sciencenews.org/view/interest/id/3/topic/Science_News_For_Kids>
- emedicine: <http://www.emedicine.com>
- *Scientific American* Online: <http://www.sciam.com>
- *New York Times*: Science section
  <http://www.nytimes.com/pages/science>

MAGAZINES

The following magazines are readily available at a local public library or bookstore. Many of these magazines also offer additional information online.

- *Make*: <http://www.makezine.com>
  Make is definitely not a common magazine, but it's a must for every inventor and student engineer. Think about the motion detector that turns on a light, the remote control for your television, smoke

alarms, and the vast number of other devices that do simple little jobs. *Make* is all about taking technology and devices that already exist and using them to make new things.

- *Odyssey* (middle school): <http://www.odysseymagazine .com>
- *Discover*: <http://discovermagazine.com>
- *Scientific American* (advanced high school scientists): <http://www.sciam.com>
- *American Scientist* (advanced high school scientists): <http://www.americanscientist.org>
- *Popular Mechanics*: <http://www.popularmechanics.com>
- *National Geographic*: <http://www.nationalgeographic.com>

EDUCATIONAL INFORMATION

Review teaching guides and materials for educators to get project ideas and discover easy-to-understand experimental methods for your own project.

- Scientific American Frontiers: <http://www.pbs.org/saf/educators.htm>
- PBS Teachers: <http://www.pbs.org/teachers/ sciencetech>
- *New York Times*: Learning Network: <http://www.nytimes.com/learning>

APPENDIX 2:
Science Supply Companies

1. **Arbor Scientific**
   P.O. Box 2750
   Ann Arbor, MI 48106-2750
   (800) 367-6695
   http://www.arborsci.com

2. **Carolina Biological Supply**
   2700 York Road
   P.O. Box 6010
   Burlington, NC 27215-3398
   (800) 334-5551
   http://www.carolina.com

3. **Connecticut Valley Biological Supply**
   82 Valley Road, Box 326
   Southampton, MA 01073
   (800) 628-7748
   http://www.ctvalleybio.com

4. **Delta Education**
   P.O. Box 3000
   80 Northwest Boulevard
   Nashua, NH 03061-3000
   (800) 258-1302
   http://www.delta-education.com

5. **Edmund Scientific's Scientifics**
   60 Pearce Avenue
   Tonawanda, NY 14150-6711
   (800) 728-6999
   http://www.scientificsonline.com

6. **Educational Innovations**
   362 Main Avenue
   Norwalk, CT 06851
   (888) 912-7474
   http://www.teachersource.com

7. **Fisher Science Education**
   4500 Turnberry Drive
   Hanover Park, IL 60133
   (800) 955-1177
   http://www.fishersci.com

8. **Frey Scientific**
   80 Northwest Boulevard
   Nashua, NH 03063
   (800) 225-3739
   http://www.freyscientific.com

9. **Nasco-Modesto**
   4825 Stoddard Road
   P.O. Box 3837
   Modesto, CA 95352-3837
   (800) 558-9595
   http://www.enasco.com

10. **Sargent-Welch/VWR International**
    P.O. Box 4130
    Buffalo, NY 14217
    (800) 727-4368
    http://www.sargentwelch.com

11. **Vernier Software & Technology**
    13979 SW Millikan Way
    Beaverton, OR 97005-2886
    (888) 837-6437
    http://www.vernier.com

12. **Wards Natural Science**
    5100 West Henrietta Road
    P.O. Box 92912
    Rochester, NY 14692-9012
    (800) 962-2660
    http://wardsci.com

GLOSSARY

ANOVA—An abbreviation for "Analysis of Variance," a statistical test that compares three or more groups.

antibiotics—Antibacterial substances produced by living organisms.

APA (American Psychological Association)—A professional society that sets a formatting and citation style commonly used in research papers.

astrophysics—The scientific discipline of the physics of stars and space.

bacteria—A kind of single-cell microorganism (organism of microscopic size) that lacks a true nucleus.

carbon dioxide—A gas produced as a by-product of respiration or combustion.

cardiac—Relating to the heart.

categorical data—Statistical term for data that are not measurable but can be assigned to a specific category.

chi-square—A statistical test designed for use with categorical data.

chronological order—Presenting something in order, following the time of occurrence.

coefficient—A mathematical term for a variable that defines a relationship between other variables.

cognitive—Relating to higher functions of the brain.

control group—A group that is compared to another, which is receiving a different treatment (the experimental group).

correlation—A way to describe the relationship between two things.

diagram—A chart, graph, or figure that illustrates data or a method.

engineering—A division of science that focuses on developing innovations to solve problems.

fungus—A type of organism that gets its energy from other organisms (either dead or alive).

graph—A chart that organizes groups of numbers into a picture for statistical or presentation purposes.

hypothesis—A plausible explanation for a scientific question; a statement that can be tested using scientific means.

IRB (Institutional Review Board)—A safety committee concerned with protecting the well-being of human research subjects.

ISEF (Intel International Science and Engineering Fair)—The largest student research competition in the world.

JSHS (Junior Science and Humanities Symposium)—A regional and national high school research competition.

mean—Represents an average score in statistical terms.

mentor—A learned teacher who provides guidance and support.

microorganisms—Organisms that cannot be seen with the naked eye, and require a microscope to be visible.

MLA (Modern Language Association)—A professional society that sets a formatting and citation style commonly used in humanities papers.

neurophysiology—The field of science that deals with the functions of the nervous system.

particle physics—The scientific discipline of the physics of subatomic matter.

perspective—View or outlook.

PhD—Doctor of Philosophy (*Philosophiae Doctor*); title held by scholars with the highest university degree.

photovoltaic cells (solar cells)—Humanmade units that harness solar energy and turn it into electricity.

plagiarism—The act of passing off as one's own the ideas or writing of another without proper credit to the original author.

probability—A statistical means of projecting the likelihood of an occurrence.

prototype—A first-generation device designed and developed by engineers.

regression line—A statistical tool used to produce the best fitting line for a set of data.

rubric—An outline used to guide evaluation of a project so that each project is scored fairly and objectively.

scatterplot—A graph of data plotted as individual points.

schematic—A design diagram commonly used by engineers.

scientific method—The scientific method involves hypothesis testing and the gathering of data through experiments.

standard deviation—Illustrates the spread of scores around an average.

statistics—A part of math dealing with the collection and analysis of data.

STS (Intel Science Talent Search)—The oldest science competition in the United States. A research competition for high school seniors who work independently, not as a team.

t-test—A type of statistical test used to compare two means.

variance—A way of showing statistical scores as they compare to the mean.

FURTHER READING

BOOKS

Bochinski, Julianne Blair. *More Award Winning Science Fair Projects.* Hoboken, N.J.: John Wiley & Sons, Inc., 2004.

Bochinski, Julianne Blair. *The Complete Handbook of Science Fair Projects.* Hoboken, N.J.: John Wiley & Sons, Inc., 2004.

Krieger, Melanie Jacobs. *Using Statistics in Science Projects, Internet Enhanced.* Berkeley Heights, N.J.: Enslow Publishers, Inc., 2002.

Rainis, Kenneth G. *Microscope Science Projects and Experiments: Magnifying the Hidden World.* Berkeley Heights, N.J.: Enslow Publishers, Inc., 2003.

Vecchionne, Glen. *100 Award-Winning Science Fair Projects.* New York: Sterling, 2001.

INTERNET ADDRESSES

The Landmark Project. "Citation Machine." 2006.
<http://citationmachine.net/>

See Appendix 1 for a list of reliable scientific sources available on the Internet.

See Chapter 10 for Internet addresses for major science competitions.

INDEX